The Teller Pasture

Claire Hamilton

iUniverse, Inc.
New York Bloomington

The Teller Pasture

iUniverse books may be ordered through booksellers or by contacting:

iUniverse
1663 Liberty Drive
Bloomington, IN 47403
www.iuniverse.com
1-800-Authors (1-800-288-4677)

ISBN: 978-1-4502-3143-5 (sc)
ISBN: 978-1-4502-3144-2 (ebk)

Printed in the United States of America

iUniverse rev. date: 6/28/2010

Contents

Table of Figures

Acknowledgements

I am indebted to Katherine Chansky, Carol Lewis and Diann Gade of the Schenectady County Historical Society, Grems-Doolittle Library, to Cindy Seacord of the Efner Historical Research Center for the use of photographs and maps from the William B. Efner collections and to Maureen Gebert, Schenectady Heritage Area Coordinator, for use of her photograph of the North Street stockade line. I wish to thank the staffs of the Schenectady County Public Library, the New York State Library, the Albany Hall of Records and the New York State Archives.

I wish to thank the staff of Hartgen Archaeological Associates, to Paul R. Huey and Joseph E. McEvoy of the New York State Department of Parks and Recreation, Division of Historical Preservation; and Ronald Kingsley, Director of the Schenectady County Community College's Community Archaeology Program for use of their archaeological studies.

I am extremely grateful to Edward Gifford, close friend of the late Axel Frieberg and executor of his estate, for his recollections of the Teller House restoration of 1976. Through his photo-journaling and note-taking efforts, I was given a rare glimpse into what lay behind the walls of an original eighteenth century hybrid Georgian home, ca. 1760. Also to be acknowledged is the late Edward (Ned) Sutton, the chief carpenter of the Teller House restoration and Marilyn Sassi, art curator and current owner of the Teller House.

Introduction

The *Teller Pasture* takes a unique look into Schenectady's past through the microcosm of the Teller pasture, a five acre plat of ground granted to Willem Teller, one of the original proprietors of the Schenectady Patent of 1664. The pasture's story will be told within the context of the history of Albany County, of which it was a part until 1809, and the colony founded by the West India Company ("GWC") in 1624. The township of Schenectady embraced a territory of 128 miles and a portion of the Mohawk valley sixteen miles long and eight miles wide. To the east, sixteen miles between Schenectady and the fire-prone Pine Barrens, was Beverwijck, a well-established trading center of the Dutch West India Company ("GWC"). To the west were found the Mohawks, the easternmost tribe of the Iroquois Confederacy—and the unknown. In 1642, on his return from a peace mission to free three captive Frenchmen from the Mohawks, as the trail wound along the ridge overlooking the site of what was to become downtown Schenectady, Arent van Curler, the chief trading agent of the Colony, first viewed the Great Flats, clothed in the bright green of Indian corn and summer crops. He wrote to his great uncle, Patroon Kilaen van Rensselaer:

> Hardly a half day's journey from the Colonie there lies the most beautiful land on the *Macquas Kil* that *eye* ever saw. ..It is impossible to reach it by boat, on account of the strong current which prevails there; and on the other hand, on account of the shallowness of the water, but I think it may be possible to reach it by wagons.[1]

Nineteen years later, with the proviso the land purchased would be transferred to representatives of the West India Company ("GWC"), he purchased the Great Flats from the Mohawk sachems (peace chiefs) of the Bear, Turtle and Wolf clans for "six hundred hands of good Wheyte Wampus, six Koates of Duffels, Thirty barrs of Lead, and nine bags of gun powder" in what would be the first major sale of land by the Mohawks to Europeans.[2] On August 27, 1664, just two months after Jacques Cortelyou, the provincial surveyor, had laid out the Schenectady lands, an English fleet of four frigates and six hundred soldiers sailed into the harbor of New Amsterdam (New York) and demanded surrender of the Colony. Since England and the Dutch Republic were then at peace, this outrageous act met with no resistance from the poorly-supplied and ill-prepared garrison and townspeople. Governor Petrus Stuyvesant's last official act was to gain lenient terms of surrender under the Articles of Capitulation, ensuring the Dutch the rights of property, religious freedom and continuance of the Dutch language and customs.[3]

Many people have been intrigued by interpretations of folklorists and writers about the nature of Schenectady's early settlement and its stockades. However, surprisingly few of these writings were based on scholarly research. As a student enrolled in the Advanced Certificate of Proficiency in Community Archaeology program, my thesis required that I delve into primary source materials relating to a historic site in the Stockade District. Dr. Ronald Kingsley, director of this unique historical archaeology program, suggested that the Teller Pasture might be a challenging topic for my archaeological research project, since it was known to be the site of the boat-building industry on the Mohawk River and of North Street "the road to the river" during the French and Indian War. There was a good possibility that my research would lead to new archaeological discoveries on the pasture. The Teller House, the red gambrel-roofed Dutch Colonial house popularly associated with the pasture, was shrouded in legend and myth as well. No one had ever attempted a 350 year title search of either the house or the pasture, but, in spite of the inherent obstacles involved, such as the dearth of traceable deeds and other legal documents, I was willing to try. As an archaeology student, I was given special access to numerous unpublished archaeological reconnaissance studies that had been done on and near the Teller pasture. In addition, I had access to the many historical repositories—the New York State Archives, Schenectady County Historical Society and the Efner Library--containing archival materials dating from the seventeenth and eighteenth centuries. Little did I know that the pasture itself would hold its own archaeological treasures that would re-define history.

My research will be guided by the following lines of inquiry: What was the relationship of the Teller pasture to the original Dutch village? What, if any, was the historical importance of the Teller pasture? Where was it located in relation to the first, second and third stockade lines? Who were the owners of the Teller pasture and what changes did they effect? What role did the Front Street houses and the signature Teller House play in the evolution of the pasture? Does the discovery of newly-identifiable archival and archaeological documentation—the only known 1756 surveyed map showing the fortifications and palisades of the second stockade, the discovery of mid-eighteenth century stockade line on North Street and access to several unpublished archaeological studies--support, or cause to be re-defined, the role of the Teller pasture in the history of the Dutch village of Schenectady?

Chapter One:
The Hudson and Mohawk Valleys Before 1664

To understand the context in which the Teller pasture evolved, it is important to be cognizant of the colonization of the Northeast before, during and after the arrival of the settlers in New Netherlands.

The Proto-Historic Period (1525-1609)

During the Proto-Historic Period (1525-1609),[4] two main native populations occupied the upper Hudson and Mohawk Valleys--the Mahicans (Mohicans), Algonquian-speaking Indians, whose sites occurred along the Hudson, north to Fish Creek in Saratoga County, westerly up the Mohawk River past Schenectady, and southerly through Columbia and Greene counties, and the Mohawks, the easternmost tribe of the Five Nation Iroquois Confederacy, whose sites were located thirty miles to the west of the confluence of the Mohawk and Hudson Rivers. The Mahicans (Mohicans), "the People of the River," were primarily foragers and fishermen. Their sites were found along the river's flood plain. The Mohawks, "the People of the Flint," were named for their hunting skills. They resided in communal longhouses, located on high, steep plateaus. Their subsistence was based mostly on farming, hunting, and the growing of maize. They traveled to hunting and fishing camps along the Mohawk.[5]

A third distinct group of native people, the Munsees, comprised of numerous sub-groups, occupied the area from the mid-Hudson Valley south to Manhattan, northern New Jersey and the western end of Long Island. They were primarily foragers and fisherman, who lived in small family groups.[6]

During the Proto-Historic Period, Basque traders from the Bay of Biscay ports in France and Spain initially established whaling stations along the Gulf of St. Lawrence, but, after 1580, the demand for furs, especially beaver, grew rapidly and trading became increasingly important. In 1604, with the ascent of Henri IV of France, a second group of traders from Normandy were given a series of monopolies along the St. Lawrence River. The most important of these was a ten-year monopoly issued to Pierre de Monts. Samuel de Champlain sailed under his auspices. Traded items included kettles made of brass, with rolled lips, small iron axes, knives and small white and indigo tubular and oval glass beads.[7]

The Independent Traders Period (1609-1624)

In 1609, Henry Hudson was hired by the East India Company ("VOC") to skipper the eighty-ton *Halve Maen* (Half Moon), with a twenty-man crew, largely Dutch. Hindered by the permanent ice north of Scandinavia from sailing around the Eurasian land mass, Hudson decided to sail west to locate a passage to the east through the North American land mass. After first exploring the Chesapeake and Delaware bays, he reached the mouth of a great river, the Hudson, (later named for him) on September 12, 1609. He sailed upriver as far as Albany, where the shallowness of the river convinced him the tidal estuary would not lead to the Pacific Ocean. However great his disappointment in not finding a Northwest Passage, he, nevertheless, had laid claim to New Netherlands for the Dutch. Hudson sailed for Europe on October 4, 1609. So important were his discoveries that, upon landing at Dartmouth, England, his logs and maps were confiscated by the British.[8]

During the Independent Traders Period (1609-1624),[9] the Dutch traded mainly from their ships and along the shoreline. In 1614, a cartel, formed to control prices and trading rights, constructed a small fort called Fort Nassau on Castle Island, about two miles south of present-day Albany. Surrounded by a moat eighteen feet wide, the plank fort had two cannon and eleven light swivel guns to defend the trade goods, furs and the dozen men of the garrison. The fort flooded in 1617 and had to be abandoned. During this time period, the Mohawk population migrated closer to the Mohawk River to have better access to this fort.[10]

The West India Company ("GWC")

In 1609, Spain was forced to agree to the "Twelve Years Truce" after failing to end their war with the Dutch. Ironically, while many Dutch opposed the truce, it allowed the Dutch a remarkable expansion of peaceful commerce, starting with the hiring of Henry Hudson, an English explorer in 1609 and ending with the granting of a charter to the West India Company ("GWC") in 1621. With a charter similar to that of the East India Company ("VOC"), the new monopoly was granted sovereign powers to build fortified trading posts and harbors, to declare war on Native inhabitants, and to conclude treaties with foreign powers.[11]

Fort Orange, the Van Rensselaer Patroonship and Beverwijck

In 1624, the newly-founded West India Company ("GWC")) built Fort Orange, a substantial structure of earth walls held in log cribbing, with platforms holding cannon to resist a possible attack from Europeans. The Company was granted exclusive and sole power to conduct the Indian trade. With the emphasis on trade, rather than settlement, food shortages developed. When war broke out in 1626 between the Mahicans (Mohicans) and the Mohawks, who lived to the west, Governor Peter Minuit (1625-1633) ordered all eighteen families settled nearby to abandon Fort Orange for the safer haven of New Amsterdam (New York). Only a garrison of a few traders and soldiers remained to defend Fort Orange.[12] To encourage settlement, the States General passed *The Privileges and Exemptions Act of 1630*, which allowed for the creation of patroonships--great manors with feudal rights and power granted. In 1631, Kilaen van Rensselaer, an Amsterdam diamond merchant and one of the Company's directors, used his insider information to hire Bastiaen Jansz Krol, Commissary at Fort Orange, to serve as his personal agent. Krol, well aware of the potential benefit of land located at the head of tidewater and near the trading post used by the Indians, secretly purchased 700,000 acres of land surrounding Fort Orange to establish van Rensselaer's patroonship (colony within a colony). In return for establishing fifty colonists within four years and for maintaining the settlers for one year, the Patroon was granted the perpetual ownership of land for himself and his heirs.[13] The purchase of such a huge tract of land on both sides of the Hudson greatly diminished the power of the Mahicans, whose territory would now lie to the south of Fort Orange in Greene County on the west, Columbia County on the east of the Hudson River.[14] The future of the fur trade would now lie to the west of the Hudson, in Mohawk territory.

In 1639, with the profits of the West India Company ("GWC")) declining, Governor Willem Kieft (1638-1647) declared a free trade zone on the Indian trade. In 1642, he sent Arent van Curler, the commissary (chief trading agent), whose duties included direction of the Colony, as well as supervision of Indian affairs in the management of the fur trade, was sent on a peace mission to the village of Ossernenon (Auriesville) to negotiate for the release of three French prisoners and to re-establish relations with the Mohawks. Although he failed in his mission to release the captives, it was largely due to this visit that a mutual agreement pact, the first of its kind, was signed the following year between the Mohawks and the Dutch. On his return trip, van Curler viewed Schenectady for the first time, describing it as a great fertile flat covered with grass and plantings of Indian corn. He wrote to his great-uncle, Kilaen van Rensselaer: "Hardly half a day's journey from the Colonie there lays the most beautiful land on the *Maquas Kil* (Mohawk River) that eye ever saw."[15] By 1645, a peace treaty had been signed with the Mohawks. In 1647, the West India Company ("GWC") replaced Governor Willem Kieft for his mismanagement of the Province and for his ill-conceived wars on the Native population. He was replaced by Governor Petrus Stuyvesant.

Conflicts inevitably arose between the Company and the agents of the Patroon (patron-proprietor). A strong-willed agent of the Colony of Rensselaerswijck, Brant van Slichtenhorst, forbade non-tenants of the Patroon to cut wood or to quarry stone on the Patroon's land. Finally, after years of petty disputes, Governor Stuyvesant (1647-1664) arrived at a decaying Fort Orange and tore down any non-company houses nearby. In 1652, he established a court and a municipal government, naming it Beverwijck (Beaver District). There were now three legal jurisdictions for the same area: the Company, the Patroon's agent, and the municipal government of Beverwijck.[16]

In 1661, Arent van Curler was granted permission to establish a new community at Schenectady for "the purpose of agriculture." On July 27, 1661, Arent van Curler signed a deed with three Mohawk sachems (civil chiefs) of the Bear, Wolf, and Turtle clans, signifying the official transfer of land at Schenectady to fifteen proprietors. Governor Stuyvesant ordered the provincial surveyor, Jacques Cortelyou, to refuse to measure off any lands until the residents signed a bond promising they would "not carry on, nor cause to be carried on, on the said Flat...any trade...with any of the Savages."[17] After nearly three years of delay, a final petition, signed by Sander Leendertse Glen, Willem Teller and Harmen Vedder was presented to Governor Stuyvesant urging the surveyor to return to lay out the farm lands and house lots.[18] No mention was made of trading rights. Having failed to secure the trading privilege, Arent van Curler, the founder of Schenectady, was not included among those who signed the appeal.[19] On June 16, 1664, the land that Arent van Curler had purchased from the Mohawk sachems became officially known as the Schenectady Patent of 1664. In 1672, the inhabitants would make a second purchase of land.

> Ye lands Lying Neare The Towne of *Schanhechtade* within three Dutch Myles in Compasse on boath Sides of ye River Westwards, Which endes in *Kinaquariones*, Where the last Battell was between The Mohoaks and the North Indians[20]

On August 27, 1664, four English frigates and a crew of 600 soldiers sailed into the harbor of New Amsterdam, demanding the surrender of the Province. Governor Stuyvesant's last official act was to gain lenient terms of surrender (in the *Articles of Capitulation*), ensuring the Dutch the rights of property, religious freedom, and the continuation of the Dutch language. In September of 1664, the *Elise*, an English warship, anchored and took possession of Beverwijck. Not a shot was fired by the soldier garrison, or by any of the 1,000 inhabitants. The surrender of the Province was complete.[21]

Chapter Two - The 17th Century Teller Pasture

Willem Teller, the Man, his Friends and Early Alliances

Willem Teller formed a lifelong bond with Alexander Lindsay Glen (known as Sander Leendertse Glen), a bond encompassing both familial and business affairs. Their association apparently went back to at least Holland and, perhaps, even Scotland. Alexander Lindsey Glen, one of the original proprietors of the Schenectady Patent, was born near Inverness, Scotland, ca. 1610, into a noble Scottish family, the Lindseys (of the Glen). When the father of Alexander Lindsay Glen, a Scottish chief, realized the price of loyalty to King Charles the First was his life and property, he convinced his son to flee across the North Sea to Protestant Holland. In Amsterdam, Patroon Kilaen van Rensselaer, one of the Directors of the West India Company ("GWC"), engaged Glen and his English wife, Catherine Dongan (known as Catherine Duncansen by the Dutch) as free colonists of his manor.[22] Glen received his commission in 1633 and served at Fort Nassau on the Delaware, where he received a land grant on the Delaware River. In 1646, he was granted land in New Amsterdam. Willem Teller, one of the original proprietors of the Schenectady Patent and a Director of the West India Company ("WIC"), was born in Holland, ca. 1620, and married Margaret Dongan (known to the Dutch as Margaret Duncansen), a sister of Glen's wife.[23] Both he and Sander Glen arrived at Fort Orange in 1639. He was appointed corporal by Governor Willem Kieft and was promoted to *Wachtmeester* (master of the watch). Like Glen, he owned property on the Delaware River, New Amsterdam, and Long Island.[24]

Although Willem Teller never resided in Schenectady, he had an alliance in the Indian trade, under the auspices of the Mohawks, with Sander Glen and Jacques Corneliese van Slyck as early as 1658. Sander Glen had acquired the Mohawk title to his land in Scotia in 1652, but did not obtain his patent from the Crown until 1665.[25]

Jacques Corneliese van Slyck, a relative of the Patroon, was the son of a high-ranking Mohawk woman, Ostoch. She is believed to have been the daughter of Jacques Hertel, a lieutenant of Samuel de Champlain, who was the first European to settle in the Mohawk Valley, and a Dutch father. Jacques Corneliese grew up in the Mohawk village of Canajoharie. He was twenty-two, when the village was settled. Jacques Corneliese became the first patentee of Schenectady. His lands were wholly exempt by the Indian proprietors.

> The lands lying between the two creeks…Stone Creek to the eastward…the Platt Creek to the westward...the lowland on the south side of the *Maques River*…40 morgens of woodlands and upland.[26]

His village lot was situated on the corner of Washington Avenue (*Handelaer's Straat*) and Front Street, where he established a tavern. The rear of his parcel fronted on the *Binne Kil*, a channel in the river separating the village and Van Slyke Island, at Cucumber Lane, a highly favorable location for the conduction of the Indian trade.

Another early lifelong bond developed between Willem Teller and Harmen Albertse Vedder. Vedder, the first settler, was a trader in Beverwijck before 1657. He shared a ½ interest in farm No. 6 with Gerrit Bancker, one of the original proprietors and a fur trader. Bancker's farm was adjacent to Teller's on the *bouwery* (farm). His house lot was adjacent to Teller's on Washington Avenue. Vedder acquired farm No. 8 on the *Bouwlandt* (arable land) in 1671--a house, 12 morgens and 130 rods, with seeds planted and buildings--for ninety whole beavers.[27] It was Harmen Albertse Vedder, Sander Glen, and Willem Teller who successfully petitioned Governor Stuyvesant for the survey of lands at Schenectady. In 1673, he was appointed one of three magistrates of Schenectady and in 1674 served as *schout* (sheriff and legal administrator, possessing both judicial and police powers) for the village. He was reprimanded on several occasions for not showing due respect to the magistrates of Willemstadt (Albany) and for pretending to the privilege of the Indian trade. His son, Harmanus, married Grietje, daughter of Jacques Corneliese van Slyck. His sons, Albert and Johannes, who were taken captive by the French during the Massacre of 1690, would marry, upon their return, into the Glen and Veeder families--Albert marrying Maria, daughter of Johannes Sanderse Glen, in 1699 and Johannes, first marrying Maria, daughter of Johannes Fort (van der Vort) in 1705, and, secondly, Engeltje, daughter of Gerrit Symonse Veeder, in 1732.[28]

Although of "Holland," Willem Teller's affairs consistently related things English to Beverwijck before 1664. As early as 1658, Teller and Glen had employed the services of an English skipper, William Thomassen, to send beaver pelts to Holland. Thomassen resided in New Amsterdam (New York). He owned property next to Paulus Schrijk. Neither Teller nor Glen ever put themselves in the debt of Dutch merchant-brokers operating in New Amsterdam. Their associate was John Willet, prominent among English merchants. When caught buying beaver pelts in 1663, the court at Beverwijck (Beaver District) ignored Willet's residency in New Amsterdam; instead, the court regarded him as a "trader from New England." Willet's partner from Boston was none other than Andries Teller, the eldest son of Willem Teller.[29]

When Margaret Dongan died in 1644, Willem Teller married a Hartford woman, Maria Varlet, the widow of Paulus Schrijk. This insured Teller of mercantile connections in Boston, Hartford, and New Amsterdam. Teller also jointly purchased Goose van Schaick's property in New Amsterdam with Rue Jacobs "just outside the water gate," and owned land on Long Island.[30]

Willem Teller's associations among Englishmen multiplied after 1664. He was living out a process of socialization to English ways that made him a valuable asset to Jeremias van Rensselaer, the fifth Patroon of the Colony of Rensselaerwijck. Teller could differentiate a good map of England from a useless one and could speak fluent English. By 1669, he had convinced Jeremias van Rensselaer to consider continuous trading arrangements with Boston, or, more specifically, with Andries Teller, his eldest son.[31]

When Albany County was created in 1683, it had no towns with corporate limits. Therefore, on November 1, 1684, Schenectady was issued a patent from Governor Thomas Dongan (Dongan Charter of 1684) in which five trustees (and their heirs) would be named as managers (grantors) of the common (undivided) land and leaders of town government. The trustees chosen were Jan van Eps, Ahasuerus Teunissen van Velsen, Ryert Schermerhorn, Willem Teller and Myndert Wemp (Wemple). The Dongan Charter gave legal form to the earlier transferral of land negotiated by the village magistrates and the Mohawks in 1672. More importantly, it became the source of all legal titles to lands embraced within 128 square miles of Schenectady subsequent to the first day of November 1684.[32] Surprisingly, no member of the Glen family was chosen as a trustee, nor were any of the original proprietors, except Willem Teller. Just one month prior to this appointment, Willem Teller had been commissioned by Governor Dongan to serve as justice of the peace for Albany County.

The Schenectady Patent of 1664

Each proprietor was given a house lot in the village plat, two *bouweries* (farms) on the Great Flats, a pasture lot in the *calver wey* (a strip of land between Front Street and the Mohawk River reserved as pasture land for the original proprietors), and a garden lot in the *laeghte* (lowland*)* west of Mill Creek and near the *Binne Kil*.[33] Willem Teller's *bouweries* on the Great Flat were described in the English Confirmatory Patent dated June 29, 1667 as:

> two pieces of land both marked No. 5, the first lying to the west of the first creek (Willem Teller's Killetje), to the east of No. 6...about 26 acres...the other lying on the hindmost piece of land by the wood side, (No. 3) to the west of No. 7, to the east of No. 1, a line cutting again from the small creek *(dove gat)*, to the woodland South west and by west...about 20 acres or 10 morgens 165 rods...as granted by Governor Stuyvesant June 16, 1664.[34]

Even prior to the official survey of the lands by Jacques Cortelyou, the French provincial surveyor, Willem Teller had contracted with Cornelis Claessen Swits to become head farmer on farm No. 5. Unfortunately, Cornelis met an untimely death when he was killed accidentally by Philip Hendrick Brouwer, the owner of the adjacent farm No. 2. in September 1663. Cornelis's son, Isaack Corneliessen Swits, and Claes Fredericksz van Petten entered into a contract of service on June 16, 1664.[35] The lessees had the use of his dwelling house, barn, hay rick, and arable land, as well as the use of his horses, geldings, mares, 102 heifers, two bull calves, and three Flemish scythes. In exchange, Willem Teller exacted a demanding rent from the lessees.

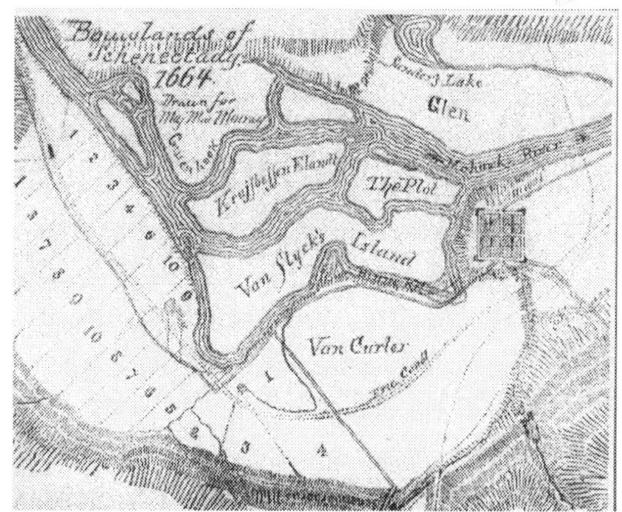

Figure 1. *Bouwlandt of Schenectady, 1664*. Drawn for Major MacMurray. Map Constructed from Actual Surveys and the Ancient Deed. Schenectady Patent, 59.

> (400) guilders in wheat to be delivered to Beverwijck, besides (40) pounds of butter additional rent…every day, plus (3) days drawing wood…but, in case of war, the lessees have none of the burden to bear.[36]

The horses, cattle, and swine roamed freely through the woods and his pasture land. For identification purposes, the horses and cattle were branded, and the hogs had their ears cut. The horses and cattle were stabled, and were provided with fodder during the winter months. Hogs were rounded up and penned in the autumn. By 1679, Teller's farm and pasture land had been enclosed with fencing. His *bouwery* now supported eight mature horses, while his number of cattle had been reduced by one-half.[37]

The Original Village

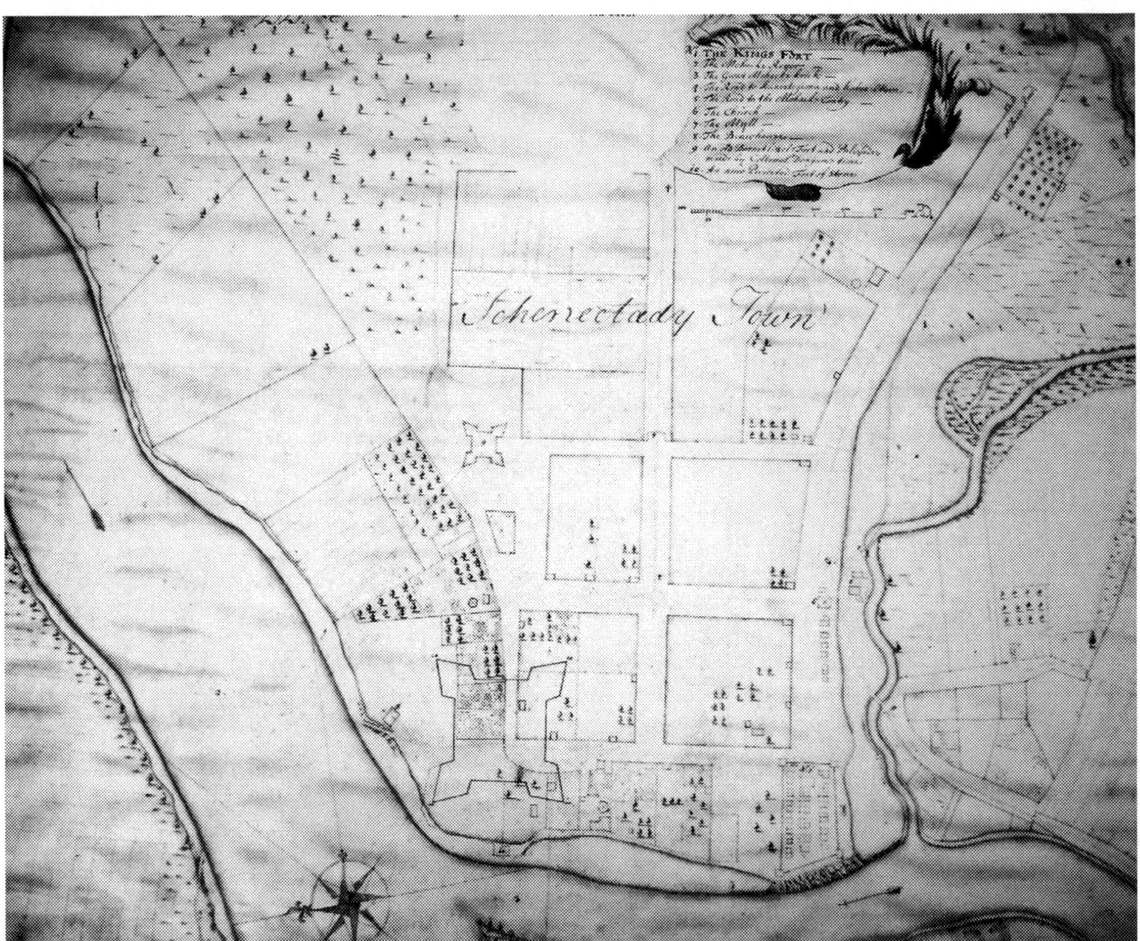

Figure 2. *The Plan de Schenectady of 1698*. Wolfgang Römer. NYS Library: Manuscripts/ Special Collections: Crown Collection.

The town was divided into a four-block quadrilateral, with four lots per block, bounded on the west by Washington Avenue, on the south by State Street, on the east by Ferry Street, and on the north by Front Street. The Teller village lot was located on the west quarter of the block bounded by Washington, Front, Church and Union Streets (see *The Plan de Schenectady of 1698*). Willem

Teller's pasture lot was located in the *calver wey*. Prior to 1703, Front Street did not extend beyond Ferry Street near the present-day St. George's Episcopal Church.

The First Stockade

The first direct documentary reference to a stockade being built around the village of Schenectady was 1680, when Jasper Danckaerts described it as a "square, set off by palisades."[38] As early as 1670, Schenectady residents were informed "they must make preparations to complete the blockhouse during the winter." The blockhouse, still incomplete, remained the sole fortification of the village. Heeding the advice of the Albany magistrates, a blockhouse was built on the northeastern corner of the stockade, on the high point of the ridge that ran across the settlement where no houses had been erected."[39] Subsequently, in 1675,

> the Commissioners and *schout* of Schenectady were ordered without delay, to have the blockhouses in your village surrounded by palisades as a place of refuge...in time of need....Not until the end of the decade would the village itself be palisaded.[40]

As late as 1687, the village was ordered fortified, and Governor Dongan proposed that a series of frontier garrisons be built in the Mohawk Valley, stretching from Schenectady to Lake Ontario "to secure the beaver and peltry trade and the King's right to the country."[41] While the upheaval associated with Leisler's Rebellion prevented the full implementation of this plan, Fort Dongan was constructed on the site where the former blockhouse, erected after 1670, had stood. Dongan's Fort would not survive the Massacre of February 8, 1690, a victim of King William's War between England and France. Fort Dongan can be identified on *The Plan de Schenectady (legend #9 an old Burnt little Fort and Palisades made by Colonel Dongan's Time).* It is important to note that the palisades line shown on Römer's *Plan de Schenectady* extended only from the Mohawk River to the Cowhorn Creek. The Map of 1698 shows a community surrounded on three sides by water: the Cowhorn Creek, the *Binne Kil* and the Mohawk River. An excerpt from the French assault on the settlement follows:

> The Town of Corlaer forms a sort of oblong with only two gates--one opposite the road we had taken;-the other leading to Orange ...Messieurs de Sainte Helene and de Mantet were to enter at the first...and which, in fact, was found wide open....M. d'Iberville and de Montesson took the left with another detachment....But they could not discover it (the gate) and returned to join the remainder of the party.... The signal of attack was given Indian fashion....M. de Mantet... reached a small fort where the garrison was under arms. The gate was burst in after a good deal of difficulty, the whole set on fire, and all who defended the place slaughtered.[42]

The French reported the loss in houses, cattle, and grain as amounting to more than four hundred thousand livres.[43] The French estimated there were eighty well-built houses in the town at the time of the massacre.[44]

Although Willem Teller was almost totally insulated from the affairs at Schenectady, he lived to see his son, Johannes, taken captive to Canada in 1690. Upon the return of his son from captivity, Willem Teller removed to New York, accompanied by all of his sons, except Johannes. Johannes took up residence in Albany until 1700.[45] On June 22, 1700, Willem Teller deeded all his lands in Schenectady to his son, Johannes, including the Teller pasture.

> certain farmlands...with title thereto...the house and lot in the Village of Schenectady...certain farmlands...with title thereto...with a lot of pasture containing two and one-half morgens (five acres) or thereabouts, between Adam Vrooman and Tryntic...extending to the *Maques river*...and a garden lot over the mill dam, with the understanding that the same shall devolve upon the children of John Teller, to be made over to the son or sons, with such compensation or satisfaction to the daughters, as he in conscience shall find to be proper.[46]

in consideration of the fact that Johannes Teller had been taken captive to Canada and his family had been impoverished. Willem Teller died in 1701.

The village remained a struggling community throughout the 1690s. It would take until 1692 to rebuild the blockhouse. The King's Fort, a temporary structure where residents lived while the settlement was being rebuilt, would not be completed until 1695. (See Figure 2. *Plan de Schenectady of 1698*). Fortunately, the French attack had left the snow-covered fields, sown with winter wheat, untouched and ready to be harvested and replanted in the spring.[47] In October 1692, the inhabitants requested relief from taxation because of their losses to the French. It was quickly granted.[48] The winter of 1691-1692 proved difficult, and that of 1697-1698 was described as the severest ever. A total of fifty heads-of-families remained in the village of Schenectady in 1697.[49]

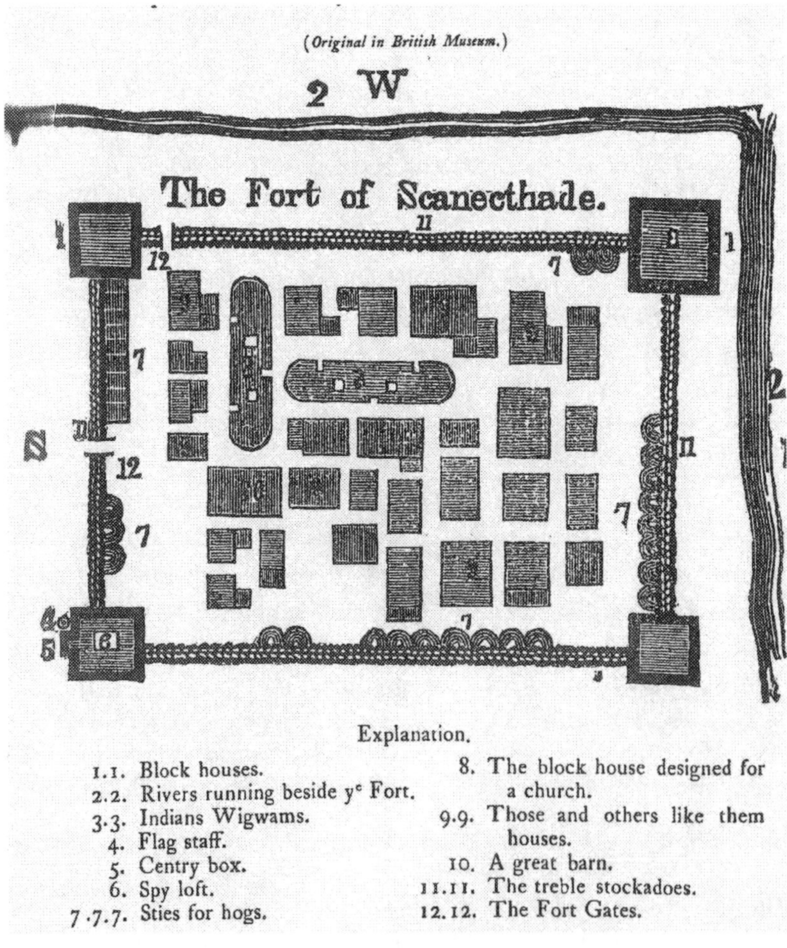

Figure 3. The King's Fort. From *A Map of Schenectady in 1695*. Drawn by the Reverend. John Miller. Schenectady Patent.

Chapter Three - The 18th Century Teller Pasture

The chief aim of the government and inhabitants after the Massacre of 1690 was to hold the village, to keep its fortifications in repair, and to maintain a sufficient garrison. Except for a few barns and houses which had been left standing and some cattle, hogs, horses, and poultry which had been found wandering in the woods, the village lay in ruins. In 1698, the government sent over Colonel Wolfgang Römer, a military engineer, to examine, report upon, and build certain forts needed on the frontier. Governor Richard Croote, Earl of Bellamont, realized the strategic importance of Schenectady and the necessity of its being fortified as a protection of the Province on the Canadian side. In spite of the urgency of the letters of the Governor of the Province to the Lords of Trade, the orders and warrants of the Provincial Council and the petitions of the chief inhabitants, all accounts of the conditions of the fortifications after 1698 show that the stockades were neglected and had been allowed to rot, rendering the town an open village. The barracks themselves were uninhabitable, and it was by no foresight of the Home government that Schenectady and its neighbors had been preserved from a second attack.[50]

In 1701, King William III granted 2,500 pounds sterling to carry out Colonel Römer's plan to fortify Albany, Schenectady and the Mohawk Valley.[51] On May 4, 1702, Queen Anne's War broke out between France and England. It was to last eleven years. In 1703, Queen Anne's Fort was built on the east angle of the stockade, on the site of the destroyed Fort Dongan. Queen Anne's Fort was constructed of heavy pine timbers and was 100 feet square, with walls twelve feet high. A blockhouse was built on each of its corners. Realizing the importance of having a British presence in the town, Lord Cornbury appointed Captain Philip Schuyler the first commandant of the Queen Anne's Fort. The fort was occupied by an original garrison of thirteen men, which was increased to forty by 1710.[52]

The Second Stockade

The construction of Queen Anne's Fort in 1703 marked the expansion of the first stockade line north to the Mohawk riverbank and to the re-routing and expansion of Front Street to the north and east of the fort. Up until now, the only known eighteenth-century map that showed the palisades of Schenectady was *A Plan of Schenectady Situated Lat. 43. Long. 74.30.* This map was commonly believed to have been based upon a sketch drawn from the memories of an unidentified British officer stationed near Schenectady towards the end of King George's War (1744-1748), or towards the beginning of the French and Indian War (1755-1763), although some historians had assigned a date as late as 1760 to it. The map was found in the New York State Library in *A Set of Plans and Forts in America: Reduced from Actual Surveys*, published by Mary Ann Rocque.[53] Now, thanks to a recent discovery of *A Geographical Plan of Schenectady*, an eighteenth century *surveyed* map, drawn by a Captain G. C. Wetterstrom, dating to September 9, 1756, the speculation has ended. We now have a much clearer and more precise snapshot of the fortifications existing at the time of the French and Indian War (1755-1763), illustrating the location of all of the blockhouses, gates and "circuits with small bastions or stockades." While North Street (the Teller pasture) cannot be specifically identified on either map, its positioning, relative to the Queen Anne's Fort and the Front Street gate, can be extrapolated by viewing a third mid-eighteenth century map, *A Map of the Town of Schenectady, (A True Copy). 1768,* by Isaac Vrooman.[54] North Street can be identified just east of the Queen Anne's Fort, as the road leading to the "Schenectady River" (Mohawk River). Governor's Lane and Ferry Street were not cut through to the Mohawk River until 1786.

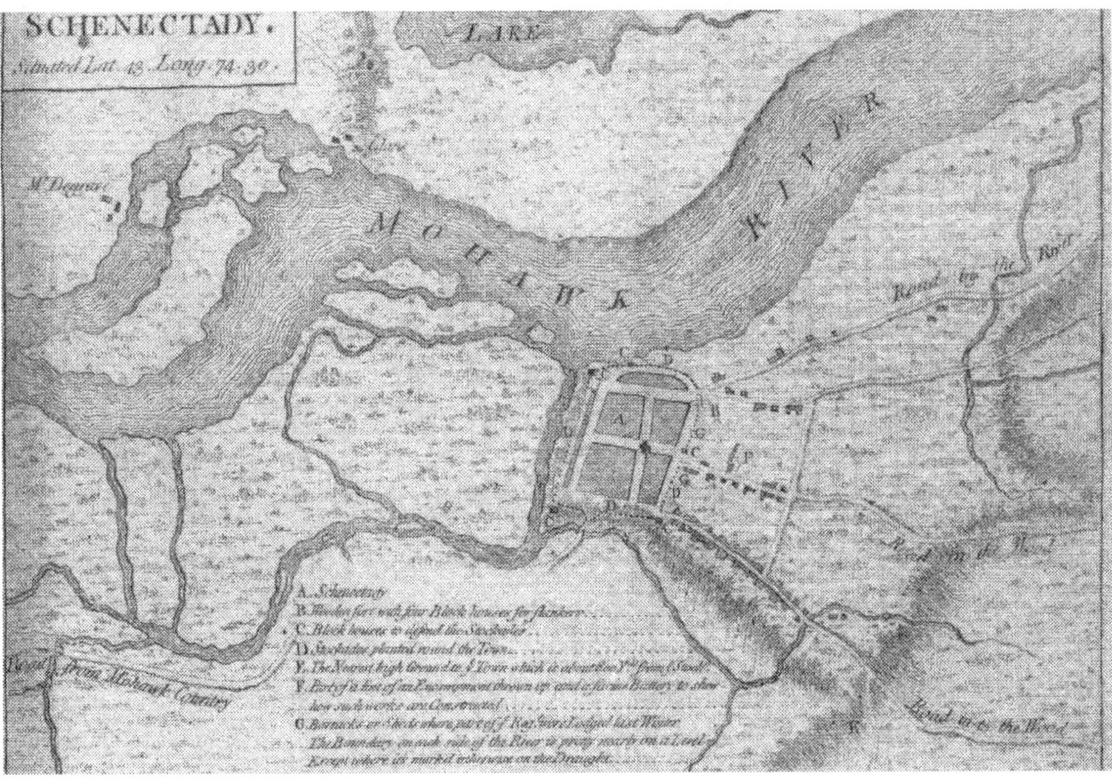

Figure 4. *A Plan of Schenectady Situated Lat. 43.Long. 74.30.* From *A Set of Plans and Forts in America: Reduced From Actual Surveys, 1763.* Mary Ann Rocque, publisher. NYS Library: Manuscripts/Special Collections

LEGEND: A. *Schenectady*; B. *Wooden fort with four Block houses for flankers*; C. *Block houses to defend the Stockades*; D. *Stockades planted round the Town*; E. *The Nearest high Ground to the Town which is about 800 yards from the Stockades*; F. *Part of a line of an Encampment, thrown up and a facine Battery to show how such works are Constructed*; G. *Barracks or Sheds where part of ye Regiment are Lodged last Winter. The Boundary on each side of the river is pretty nearly level except where it is marked otherwise on the Draught.*

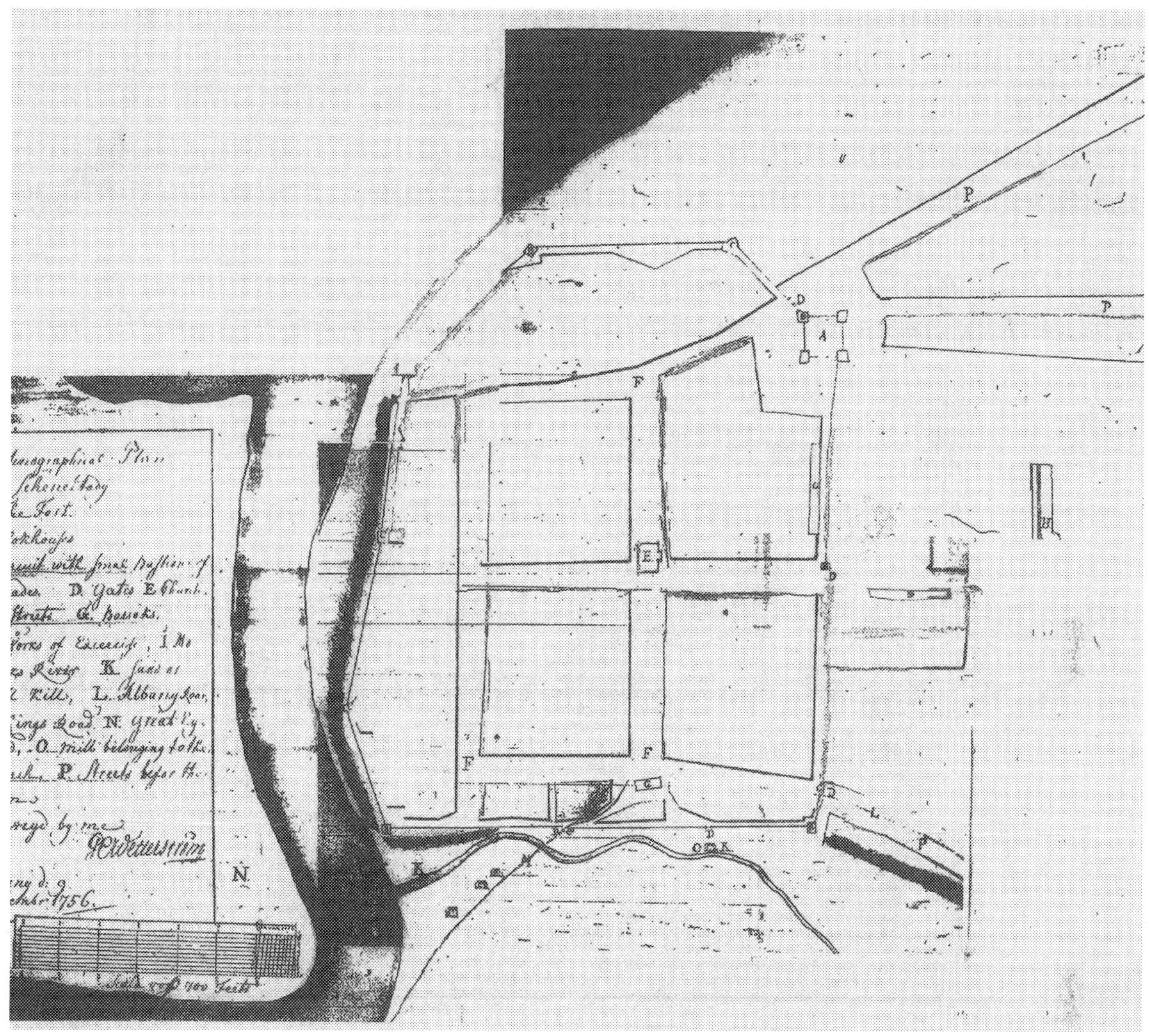

Figure 5. *A Geographical Plan of Schenectady.* Captain G. C. Wetterstrom, surveyor. 9 September 1756. NYS Library: Manuscripts/Special Collections Section.

LEGEND: A. *The Fort*; B. *Blockhouses*; C. *Circuits with small bastions or stockades*; D. *Gates*; E. *Church*; F. *Streets*; G. *Barracks*; H. *Works of Exercise*; I. *Mohawk River;* K. *Land of Mill Kill*; L. *Albany Road*; M. *Kings Road*; N. *Great Island [Van Slyck Island]*; O. *Mill belonging to the Church*; P. *Streets before the Town.*

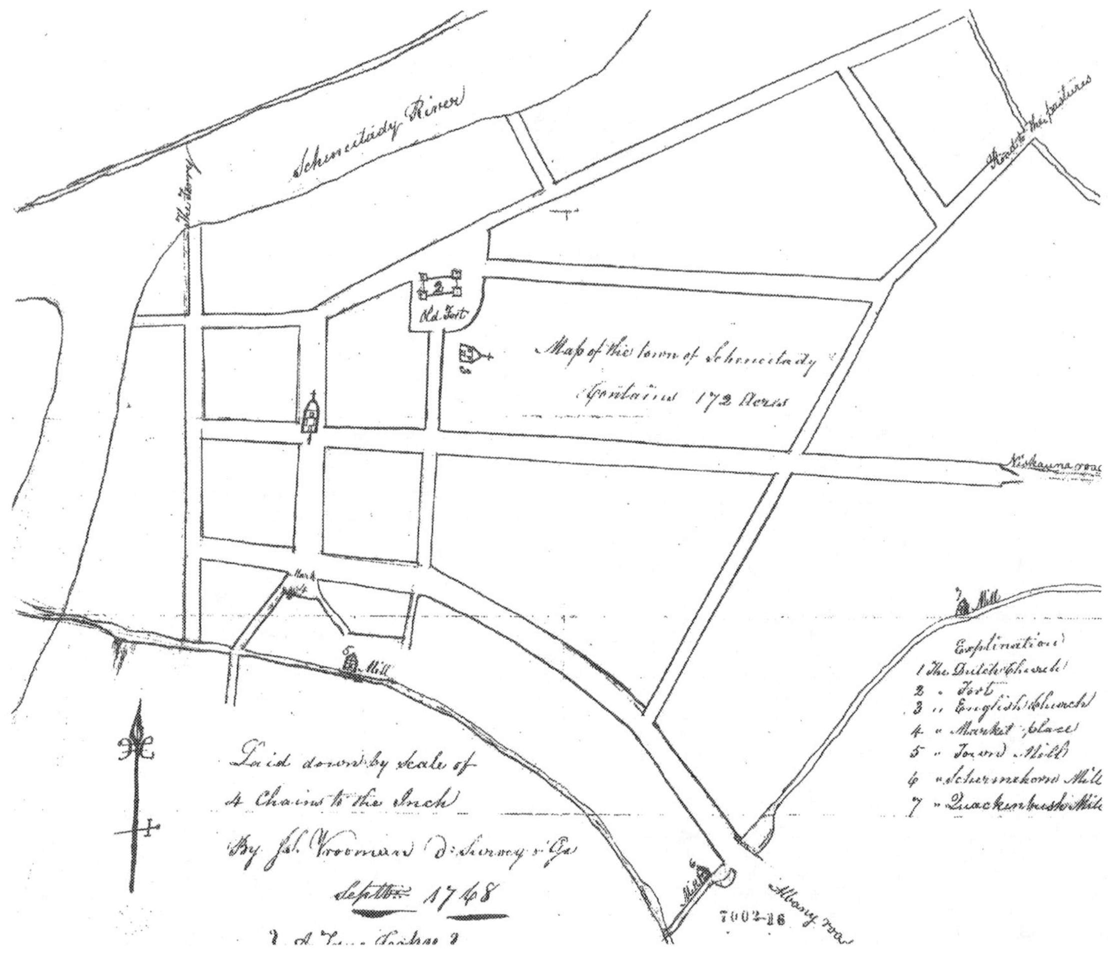

Figure 6. *Map of the Town of Schenectady: 1768 (A True Copy).* Isaac. Vrooman. NYS Library: Willis T. Hanson Collection. *EXPLANATIONS*: 1. *Dutch Church.* 2. *The Fort.* 3. *The English Church.* 4. *The Market place.* 5. *The Town Mill.* 6. *The Schermerhorn Mill.* 7. *The Quackenbush Mill.*

Johannes, Son of Willem, Inherits the Pasture (1700-1725)

As the sole inheritor of Willem Teller's Schenectady lands, Johannes took up residence in Schenectady after 1700. With the death of Willem Teller in 1701, four of the five trustees named in the Dongan Charter of 1684 had died, leaving the common (undivided) lands under the management of Ryert Schermerhorn, the only surviving trustee. The trustees held title to Schenectady real estate and granted perpetual leases, reserving quitrents, but no one knew for whom they acted. They alone had the power to call town meetings and the law required them to obtain a warrant from a justice of the peace before doing so. In spite of the granting of a second patent on February 17, 1702, Ryert Schermerhorn paid no regard to the new charter, or to the newly-elected trustees. He continued to "act solely" and was charged repeatedly with "mismanagement and breach of trust."[55] Col. Peter Schuyler and Johannes Glen, two of the newly-named trustees, petitioned the governor for an amended charter, citing the Dongan Charters of 1684 and 1703. An amended charter was granted in 1705, omitting Schermerhorn's name. However, the legal battle did not end there. Schermerhorn continued to remain as sole trustee until May 25, 1714, when he was "fully suspended."[56] The Dongan Charter of 1684 and 1714 followed the *Law of Primogeniture* (inheritance by the first-born son). Therefore, Johannes Teller, as heir of Willem Teller, was named as one of the new trustees of the 1714 Charter.[57] The Dongan Charters clearly benefited the early settlers and their relatives, who were generally granted lucrative patents. In defense of their control of the nearly 80,000+/- acres of land, plus political control of the village, the trustees argued they were obligated to follow the English law. However, the English had granted the Dutch the option of following Dutch inheritance customs, as spelled out in *The Articles of Capitulation*, signed at the time of surrender of the Province.[58]

On March 25, 1718, the trustee, Ryert Schermerhorn, although officially suspended in 1714, along with John Wemp, and Arent Bradt, granted Patent No. 17, *Poenties Kil and Mill*, to Johannes Teller, Johannes Vedder, and Tunis Clawson, transferring sixty-two acres of woodland, including a saw mill and creek, to them. Patent No. 17 was adjacent to Teller's farm No. 5. The patent also conveyed additional rights and privileges, in return for a minimal rental every year.

> Shall have free liberty of cutting and carrying away any saw logs...fencing and digging and carrying away any stones...for a yearly rental of 30 good merchantable deal boards in lieu of all other rents...due on the 25th day of March, every year.[59]

Johannes Teller continued to use the pasture for the grazing of animals, the boarding of livestock and the cultivation of crops. *The Plan de Schenectady of 1698* depicted a village surrounded by land already under cultivation. Johannes Teller made his will May 15, 1725. He died May 28, 1725. He devised to his first-born son, Johannes:

> a parcel of land at Schenectady, No. 3, being the hindmost parcel, to the west of No. 7, and to the east of No.1 containing about 20 acres or 10 morgens and 260 rods, with all the pasture and upland, also my third interest in the sawmill.[60]

Johannes, Son of Johannes, Inherits the Pasture (May 28, 1725 -1744)

When Johannes Teller, the eldest son of Johannes, inherited the pasture, a brief period of peace had prevailed, but, by the time he died in 1744, King George's War (1744-1748) would be declared. It is likely that the pasture continued to support the agricultural needs of the community and the Colony, but there is evidence that the pasture's riverbank was taking on a life of its own. The strict guidelines that pasture land be solely devoted to the grazing and housing of animals had long since been ignored. For the Dutch, water meant trading and the access to the Indian trade which, although banned in Schenectady, had been their main impetus for settlement.

When Johannes Teller died unmarried in 1744, William Teller, his brother, inherited the easterly third of the pasture, extending from Front Street to the Mohawk River. Maria Glen, his sister, inherited a sizeable portion of the middle third of the pasture, excepting two releases to Johannes's nieces, Susanna Vedder and Susanna Glen. On July 1744, shortly before his death, Johannes transferred the house lot at 57 Front Street (113 Front Street after 1888), comprising the westerly third of the pasture, to William Schermerhorn, son of his late sister, Margareta

Schermerhorn. The lot, measuring 65 feet frontage, 660 feet depth, extended from Front Street to the Mohawk River.[61]

The lot devised by Johannes to his niece, Susanna Vedder, by release of Maria Glen, was made on October 9, 1744. The lot devised to his niece, Susanna Glen, by release of Abraham and Maria Glen, did not occur until April 11, 1754. It appears that the timing of this release to Susanna Glen was delayed until she had married and reached the age of majority.[62] These two releases allowed for the creation of North Street on April 13, 1754.

> By release from Nicholas van Petten and Susanna, his wife, niece of Johannes Teller, deceased, and Abraham van Eps release to Abraham Fonda. A lot on the east side of the lot of William Schermerhorn, which Nicholas van Petten, Susanna, his wife, and Abraham van Eps and William Teller have granted for a common street, by virtue of a release made by Susanna, wife of Nicholas Van Petten, by her uncle, Johannes Teller, deceased, by Abraham van Eps, by virtue of a release from Maria Glen, by brother Johannes Teller, 9 October 1744, and to Abraham van Eps, by release of Abraham Glen and Maria Glen, his wife, 11 April 1754.[63]

The release made by Nicholas van Petten and Susanna, his wife, to Abraham Fonda of the river lot on April 11, 1754, reads:

> All that lot of land on the east side of the lot of William Schermerhorn, bounded as follows: North by the bank of the river, then along the bank to the lot of William Schermerhorn, 53' to the lot of Joseph Yates, then along the lot of Joseph Yates to the new street.[64]

The Yates parcel appears to have existed on the west side of North Street well prior to Johannes Teller's death. Only the middle third of the pasture, minus the three contiguous lots near the Mohawk River, remained undivided as of 1754; the Front Street lots west of North Street—61 Front Street (117 Front Street), 63 Front Street (119 Front Street), and 65 Front Street (121 Front Street)--were, in all likelihood, subdivided before 1754, but no exact date can be determined. William Schermerhorn's house lot at 57 Front Street (113 Front Street) was subdivided in July 1744.

William Teller, Johannes's brother, made his will April 1752, but did not die until 1757. Johannes Schoonmaker, a farmer and stepson of William Teller, inherited a fifty-foot strip of pasture land east of North Street, extending from Front Street to the Mohawk River. William Teller's son, Jacobus, a merchant, inherited the rest of the *weyland* (first land) east of North Street, extending from Front Street to the Mohawk River.[65] On April 13, 1754, a fifteen-foot strip of this was dedicated for the creation of North Street. Two years after William Teller's death, Johannes Schoonmaker and Jacobus Teller merged their lands to create three 220-foot lots abutting North Street. On May 8, 1759, they sold their interests in the pasture to Joseph C. Yates, Jr., a blacksmith, and future father-in-law of Jacobus Teller.[66] Joseph C. Yates Jr. then sold a portion of this land to his father-in-law, Jellis Fonda, a carpenter, on July 6, 1759. His son-in-law, Cornelius Peek, a wheelwright, was deeded the river parcel east of North Street.[67]

The Front Street Lots West of North Street

What do the records show regarding the Front Street lots west of North Street? While the lots east of North Street passed down through the Yates family and remained undeveloped until close to the end of the eighteenth century, the lots west of North Street were improved with three houses that date back to the 1750s or earlier. However, no recorded mortgages or deeds appear until May 1, 1782 when Johannes Cuyler, a descendant of an old patrician family of fur traders from Albany and a cousin of the Glens, transferred the Adam Vrooman House at 63 Front Street to Cornelius P. van Slyck, great-grandson of Jacques Corneliese van Slyck and cousin of Jesse van Slyck. The lot measured 42 feet 6 inches by 118 feet, with a rear dimension of 38 feet 6 inches, all English measure. It was bounded "on the west by Claas Veeder (son of Pieter Veeder and great-grandson of Simon Volkertse Veeder, an original proprietor), on the east by Jesse van Slyck and on the north by Abraham van Eps."[68] In 1763, Johannes Cuyler married Susanna Vedder, the widow of Nicholas A. van Petten and only daughter of the late Harmanus Vedder and Annetje Teller.[69]

Cornelius P. van Slyck, son of Pieter van Slyck, married Catarina P. Veder (Vedder) on March 30, 1764. Like his cousin, Jesse van Slyck, he is best known for his exemplary service in the Revolutionary War. On May 29, 1775, he was appointed ensign in the Continental Service under Captain Cornelius van Dyck for duty at Ticonderoga. He served in the Canadian campaign, taking part in the siege of St. John's. On March 1, 1776, he signed an agreement with Philip Schuyler for service at Lake George and Ticonderoga, and by April 24, 1777, he was in command of a detail of forty-five men for duty between Albany and Lake George.[70]

No recorded mortgages or deeds appear for 65 Front Street until March 1783 when Deborah Sanders and John Sanders Jr., the mortgagees of the property, sold the Teller House to Jesse van Slyck as part of the settlement of the estate of John Sanders. John Sanders is best known for his marriage in December 1739 to Deborah Glen, Colonel Jacob Glen's only child. In 1765, he became the sole owner of the Glen estate by buying out the interests of John Glen of Albany and of John Glen Jr. of Schenectady. His ties can be traced back to Thomas Sanders, an English émigré who sought political asylum in Holland. In 1636, Thomas Sanders received a patent from Governor Kieft for a house and 25 morgens of land in Manhattan. His son, Robert Sanders, became the first agent the van Rensselaer directors had in this country. Although of English origin, he was a Dutchman by language, education and sympathy. He served as mayor of Albany, but always remained an agent, financier and head citizen of Albany. Barent Sanders, John Sander's father, also served as mayor from 1750-1754.[71] John Sanders was commissioned in 1747 as captain of one of Schenectady's five militia companies. He was one of twenty-three men designated by Arent Bradt (the last surviving trustee of the Dongan Charter of 1714) in his will to serve as a trustee of the common lands. John Sanders died September 13, 1782. His will was probated February 7, 1783. In addition to his vast holdings in the Glen-Sanders estate, John Sanders left real estate in Schenectady to his five children. He left a dwelling house on Washington Avenue where he lived and

> A pasture ground lying to the east of Schenectady to the north of the street (Front Street) that leads to Canistigajone, where David Rouse now lives...also, a house and lot lying in Schenectady on the north side of the street that leads direct from the Dutch church to Canistigajone.[72]

The Teller House has often been referred to as "the house that Jesse van Slyck built." However, the records clearly indicate that he did not acquire 65 Front Street until March 14, 1783. The terms for repayment of his mortgage read as follows:

> Jesse van Slyck, for and in consideration of a sum of 145 pounds, 8 shillings and 8 pence, Gold or Silver, HATH MORTGAGED all that certain house and lot of ground (65 Front Street) situate lying and being in the Town of Schenectady on the east side of the street or the way that leads to Jacob Fonda, is butted and bounded South by the said street, West by a lot of Cornelius P. van Slyck, North by the lot of the heirs of Abraham van Eps, and east by the street that leads to the river...containing in breadth South by the said street 40'east by the street that goes to the river, one hundred and eighteen feet, and by the lot of the said van Eps thirty nine feet and one half, all English measure, provided always and upon condition that if the said Jesse van Slyck, his heirs, executors and administrators do well and truly pay or cause to be paid unto the said Deborah and John Sanders, their Heirs, Executors, Administrators and assigns the aforesaid sum of seventy two pounds, fourteen shillings and four pence ...with lawful interest for the same on or before the day or time herein before.[73]

In legend and myth, no one had been more closely identified with the Teller House than Jesse van Slyck. Jesse van Slyck was historically known as a "larger-than-life" patriot of the Revolutionary War. Some of his heroic feats include commanding a detail which marched to Saratoga in April 1777, where his unit joined four hundred of the Vermont militia under Colonel Seth Warner and proceeded to Jessup's Patent; commanding a company throughout the campaign against General Burgoyne; and in April 1778, commanding part of a company which joined a detachment of one hundred and twenty-five whites and a few Indians under Major Abraham Swits in apprehending Tories at Beaverdam. From 1780-1782, he served at Fort Plain, Stone Arabia and Fort Herkimer.[74] On a more personal level, Jesse van Slyck was infamously known as a "drinking man" who drove his wife crazy by his unkindness's. Those who believe Jesse van Slyck built the Teller House cite as evidence writings from *The Diary of Harriet Bowers Mumford Paige*. The diary is a third-person account of families who lived in the stockade. It is based on the memories of Harriet Bowers Mumford Paige's Aunt Eatie (Margaret Swits Vrooman) who was born in the 1780s. The diary was written ca. 1860 and is not dated. The following are two excerpts of what Harriet Paige wrote about Jesse van Slyck and the red gambrel-roofed brick house (65 Front Street).

> Old Lewis Barhydt lived opposite the red brick house on the corner of Front and North Lane, where Marten van Slyck lived. Marten van Slyck sold the red brick house to Robert Logue. This must have been 1807, 1808, 1809 or 1810.[75]

> Old Jesse van Slyck, who married Jacomyntje Groot, built the old brick (red brick) house....must have lived there in 1795 or long before and in 1806....Marten van Slyck never lived in the old brick house.[76]

Harriet Paige's writings are fragmentary and inconsistent, at best. Her writings fail to shed any light on who built the Teller House. In addition, her Aunt Eatie's recollections can only be traced back to 1795. As for the argument that "Jesse van Slyck, who married Jacomyntje Groot (in 1762) built the old brick house," following a custom of early Dutch settlers who built houses prior to their weddings, it must be noted that several direct descendants of Willem Teller were also married in the early 1760s. John Sanders Glen, son of Maria Teller and Abraham Glen, married Sara Sanders, daughter of Deborah Glen and John Sanders, in September 1762; John Cuyler married Susanna Vedder, daughter of Annetje Teller and Harmanus Vedder, in July 1763 and Jacobus Teller, son of William Teller, married Maria Yates in November 1762.[77]

The Tax Legislation of 1799 (Amended in 1801)

Legislation enacted in 1799 established a standardized system of assessing and taxing real and personal estates. Each roll required the name of possessor (owner) of real or personal property; the description of the real estate; the value of real estate; the value of the personal estate; total assessed value; and the amount of county, state and poor taxes due. Prior to this, tax rolls consisted of a "name and total value" only. There was no way of determining what residents owned, where they owned it, or whether what they owned was part of their real or personal estate. Fortunately, several of these standardized rolls still exist and have been preserved by the New York State Archives. In the absence of deeds, these rolls prove to be an invaluable aid in verifying the ownership of property in the latter years of the eighteenth century and in the early years of the nineteenth century. Insofar as the ownership of the Teller House is concerned, the rolls show that the last year Jesse van Slyck owned the Teller House was in 1799. His son, Marten van Slyck, became the owner of record in 1800. In 1801, the ownership of the Teller House transferred to Cornelius van Vranken. Subsequent rolls and deeds revealed that Robert Logue never owned 65 Front Street, as Harriet Paige believed.[78]

The Tax List of 1766

What, if anything, can be learned from the Tax List of 1766 regarding the ownership of the Teller House? Although the Tax List of 1766 was limited in description to "name and total value (in pounds sterling)," it is worth analyzing, since it would have been published close in time to the date the red gambrel-roofed house would have been built. It is reasonable to assume that the owner of the Teller House would have come from the greater-patrician or elite class (median assessment: 60 pounds), or at least from the lesser-patrician class (median assessment: 24 pounds), based on the 1783 purchase price of 145 pounds, 8 shillings and 8 pence gold paid for the Teller House.[79] This price was fully three times the purchase price of 43 pounds sterling paid for the Adam Vrooman House in 1782.[80] The assessed values of the Teller descendants on the 1766 Tax List were as follows: John Sanders, the former owner of the house prior to his death in 1782, had an assessed value of 194 pounds sterling. This value would have included his many holdings in the township of Schenectady. Abraham Glen (Maria Teller) had an assessed value of 56 pounds sterling; John Cuyler Jr. (Susanna Vedder) had an assessed value of 60 pounds sterling; the heirs of Niklaas van Petten had an assessed value of 30 pounds sterling; William Schermerhorn, nephew of Johannes Teller, had an assessed value of 16 pounds sterling; and Abraham van Eps Jr. had an assessed value of 12 pounds sterling. Jesse van Slyck and Cornelius van Slyck, by comparison, had very low assessed values of 2 pounds sterling each; it is highly doubtful that either of them owned real estate in 1766.[81]

The Origins of the Front Street Houses

There has been much debate regarding the Front Street houses--when they were built and who built them. In the 1950s and 1960s, a Committee on Historical Markers was formed to identify structures built in the Stockade district prior to 1825. According to Neil Reynolds, the principal objective of the committee was not necessarily to identify original owners and ascertain actual age. Each house was considered separately, with no consideration given to neighboring structures. The Committee on Historic Markers designated 119 Front Street as the Adam Vrooman House (ca. 1720), based on a 1726 deed from Adam Vrooman to Jan Vrooman, his son. Although the deed mentions a "house with a kitchen thereon," the lot described would not have placed the Adam Vrooman House at its current location within the Teller pasture. The Committee assigned a date of 1720 as the year built, based on "the architecture of the gable-end-to-street two-story Dutch house and kitchen thereon." Its early eighteenth-century features include heavy 12 inch by 14 inch foundation beams, clapboard siding and sturdy hand-hewn framing. The original eighteenth-century house measured 20 feet by 20 feet. The house was extended easterly at a later date.[82]

Figure 7. The Adam Vrooman House. C. Hamilton. 2007.

The Committee designated 113 Front Street, as the William Schermerhorn House (ca.1785). They believed the English bond brickwork and the general architecture of the two-story center hall house with gables on the side suggested a construction date of 1785.[83]

Figure 8. The William Schermerhorn House. 1962 National Registry photo. Courtesy of Schenectady County Historical Society.

The Committee designated 121 Front Street as the Johannes Teller House (ca. 1740), citing the being clause of Deed Book "C," Page 588, 5 November 1817 "as being the same house and lot sold to William Schermerhorn in July of 1744." However, the abutting owners referenced in Deed Book "C," Page 588: "west by the heirs of Adam S. Vrooman, east by the lot of Jeremiah Fuller" clearly would place the referenced Johannes Teller House as being located on the Schermerhorn parcel (113 Front Street).[84]

Figure 9. The Teller House. Union Star photo, September 28, 1954. Notation: Built by Barent Vrooman (ca. 1752). Courtesy of Efner Library.

Figure 10. The Teller House. Baldwin photo. Historic American Building Survey, 1937. Notation: Built by Barent Vrooman (ca. 1752). Courtesy of Efner Library.

Figure 11. The Teller House. L. B. Sebring, Jr., 1958. Notation: Built by Barent Vrooman (ca. 1752). Courtesy of Efner Library.

Does this rule out the possibility that the red brick gambrel-roofed house at the corner of Front and North Streets could be the original Teller House? Not necessarily. A closer examination of the structure of the house reveals that the framework of the center hallway and the easterly wing were constructed during the early decades of the eighteenth century. The roof has a high steep gable in the Dutch style and the floor plan of the original structure is that of an early Dutch floor plan. The hallway reveals evidence of a jamb less, hooded fireplace with open sides. These features were incorporated into the hybrid one-and-one-half-story Dutch Colonial (Georgian-style) house built in the 1760s.[85]

The house, purchased by Jesse van Slyck on March 14, 1783, was very similar in style to that of the John Pruyn House, with flaring roof eaves, shed dormers, paneled shutters, and decorative brickwork over the lintels. In nearly all outward appearances, the Teller House owes its style to the influence of New England Georgian architecture, with virtually the only remaining Dutch characteristics being the "weather-boarded" west gable end and the steeply-pitched staircase with high risers and overhanging treads, which led to the attic or garret. A split Dutch door, with six bulls-eye glass sections located above, opens to a center hallway. A door to the left of the center hallway opens to the dining room, which is the room where the residents would have done most of their living. A Georgian fireplace, with paneling, brick jambs and Delft tile surround, date the house as being built in the 1760s.[86] Other Georgian-style features of this period include the high, plaster-covered ceilings with no beams exposed, and the gray-green colored trim favored in Anglo-Dutch houses of that period. The original roof would have been wood-shingled or made of stone, with three Dutch-styled shed dormers on both the front and rear roofs. Just such a roof, extending over the front steps, was in evidence when the shingles were removed during the restoration in 1976.[87]

Figure 12. The Pruyn House. From *Colonial Homes* 12, no. 4 (July-August 1986).

It was theorized that the living room of the Georgian house originally served the same function as front rooms in conventional urban Dutch houses--as a place of business, or as a shop--and that the window to the east side of the front door was originally a second entranceway leading directly into the living room from Front Street. However, Edward Sutton, the chief carpenter of the restoration of 1976, disputes this finding that a second entranceway led directly into the living room.[88] However, there is evidence on the east gable end that an opening has been bricked over. The Federal-style fireplace with a Delft tile surround is estimated to have been added in the late 1780s or early 1790s. It is believed that the brick lean-to addition, extending across the rear of the house (jutting four feet westerly from the west wall of the original structure) was built at or about the same time, based on the Federal-style fireplace in the kitchen. A beehive oven abutted the Federal-style fireplace on the exterior. The lean-to addition encroached onto Cornelius P. van Slyck's lot by an additional four feet. The east wall of the brick lean-to addition paralleled the angle of North Street. The American bond brick lean-to addition measured approximately 41 feet by 15 feet.

The Remaining Acreage West of North Street

What became of the remaining vacant land on the west side of North Street? It appears that John Sanders Glen, the son of Maria Teller and Abraham Glen, probably inherited a sizeable share of the pasture from his father. In an 1813 deed, he is documented as the owner of record of a lot bordering 63 Front Street and 65 Front Street on the north.[89] In another deed filed in 1839, he is cited as formerly "conveying an undivided half-interest in a lot on the west side of North Street to Abraham van Eps, Mary Young and Eve Young, heirs of Abraham van Eps".[90]

Upon the death of Abraham Glen, John S. Glen sold his father's interest in the Glen estate to his cousin, Debora Glen, then wife of John Sanders. When John Sanders died, John S. Glen again inherited a sizeable interest in the Glen estate through the inheritance of his wife, Sara Sanders. He had married Sara Sanders, his cousin, and daughter of Debora Glen and John Sanders, on September 11, 1762. John S. Glen also was appointed administrator of Abraham van Eps's estate when the named executors, his sister, Susanna, and his niece "refused to act."[91] He is listed on both the 1813 and 1816 Assessment Rolls as the owner of land on North Street.[92]

By the mid to late eighteenth century, six houses were present on the Teller pasture. Four of the houses were located on Front Street west of North Street; there was a house located on the south bank of the Mohawk on the William Schermerhorn parcel, and one located on the former Yates parcel, abutting the river parcel of Nicholas van Petten. On May 13, 1794, Volkje Veeder, a cousin of Catarina Veeder, Cornelius P. van Slyck's wife, purchased 63 Front Street from Alexander Ellice, a London merchant. Although Alexander Ellice was the mortgagee of 63 Front Street, it is not clear whether he actually owned the parcel or just arranged the financing for it. Alexander Ellice, a Scot, was a partner in the Phyn and Ellice Fur Trading Company, located on the northeast corner of Union Street and Ferry Street. He resided at 205 Union Street (the present day English Garden Bed and Breakfast). During the Revolutionary War, he sold his interests in the Union Street property to John Sanders, a wealthy loyalist sympathizer, and fled to England. [93] The lot measured 42 feet 6 inches frontage on Front Street, with a rear dimension of 38 feet 6 inches. The east side dimension measured 114 feet 2 inches, reflecting the encroachment of Jesse van Slyck's lean-to addition.[94] Volkje Veeder was the daughter of Simon, son of Volkert Symonse, and great-granddaughter of Simon Volkertse Veeder, an original proprietor. Her mother was Margriet, daughter of Barent Wemp.[95]

North Street, Boat Building, and the French and Indian War (1755-1763)

From the days of the Mohawk canoes and dugouts and those of the first Indian traders, the river was the artery of trade between the east and far west. After Schenectady was settled in 1661, the flat-bottomed "scow skiff," propelled by oars, made its appearance. From this evolved the larger flatboats or bateaux, propelled by oars, poles, and sails, which appeared on the Mohawk about

1725. These boats carried from one to two tons, their size being determined by the number of land carries required on the river trip.

Merchants and military commanders, forced to travel overland from Albany due to the natural barrier of the Cohoes Falls, had found an ideal harbor in the *Binne Kil*, a sluggish, slack water channel, protected from the force of the main current of the Mohawk. Boatbuilding followed as a natural consequence, with boatyards spread along the riverbank between Washington Avenue and North Street. This area became known as the "Strand Street/River." As the need to move heavier freight and ordinance upriver increased, the "Strand Street/River" became the site for the construction and staging of hundreds of bateaux attached to military expeditions during King George's War (1744-1748), the French and Indian War (1755-1763), and the Revolutionary War (1776-1783). These bateaux were in general use until 1795, when the building of locks and canals by the Inland Lock Navigation Company at Little Falls, German Flats and Rome, made larger boats possible. The Durham and Schenectady boats of ten tons burden appeared--poles, oars, and sails, being their propelling forces.

Figure 13. Durham Boat. From *A History of the County of Schenectady, N.Y. From 1662 to 1886.*

The Durham boat was similar to a modern canal boat, broad, flat-bottomed and straight-sided, with easy lines at the bow and the stern to help its flotation on striking a rapid. This led to a golden-age of boat building on the "Strand Street/River." Judge John Sanders, in his history of the county in the war of 1812, noted it was no uncommon sight to see from twenty-five to one-hundred boats on the stocks at the boatyards, extending from near the Mohawk Bridge to North Street. The boats that conveyed the army of General Wilkinson down the St. Lawrence were all built at this place, the oak forests furnishing the requisite material.[96]

The principal boat builders were the van Slycks, Marselises, Veeders, and Peeks, many of whom came from Dutch families with strong Mohawk connections.[97] All of these principal boat building families, who were descendants or in-laws of the Tellers or Glens, either owned property or resided upon the Teller pasture during the eighteenth century.

With the declaration of King George's War in 1744, three-thousand pounds was voted for placing the frontier posts in attitudes of defense. Intelligence had found its way into the Province that the French intended to invade the Province from Canada, with fifteen-hundred veterans and one-hundred Indians. Colonel Schuyler and Major Collins were obliged to suspend the construction of six planned blockhouses, due to ongoing assaults from Indians in the employ of France. Because of the imminent danger of such raids, two-hundred men from the militias of

Suffolk, Queens, Westchester, Dutchess, Ulster, and Orange counties, were recruited to increase and to strengthen the garrisons at Saratoga and Schenectady.[98]

In the spring of 1746, thirteen-thousand pounds was voted for the defense of the Province. As tensions intensified, the Assembly enacted a law whereby ship carpenters, house carpenters, joiners, sawyers, and all artificers and laborers were arbitrarily pressed into public service. Horses, and wagons, which could tend to the invasion, were placed at the discretion of the officers entrusted with the management of the enterprise. By 1747, there were two companies stationed at Schenectady: one at Fort Hunter; and one between Fort Hunter and Schenectady. On the eighth of April 1748, the Assembly passed a law authorizing the inhabitants of Schenectady, to construct two block-houses for their defense.[99]

On April 13, 1754, North Street was cut through for the hauling of timber to the riverbank from the edge of the pine forest that bordered the town. North Street was directly accessible from Front Street, just east of the Queen Anne's Fort. Governor's Lane and North Ferry Street would not be cut through until after the Revolutionary War.[100] Carpenters, masons, sawyers, wheelwrights, ship joiners, turners, blacksmiths and teamsters were again called upon to construct hundreds of bateaux and wagons for the transportation of provisions and ordinances. A merchant, chosen to purchase local agricultural products and to arrange for their transport from Albany to Schenectady, reported that two-thousand five-hundred-eighteen wagonloads had been hauled to the North Street riverfront.[101]

At the beginning of the French and Indian War (1755-1763), the Assembly passed an act for raising three-thousand pounds to be expended in fortifying the village, but after the fall of the French power in Canada, it was reported that the defenses of the village fell into decay and were absent at the outbreak of the Revolutionary War. The Queen Anne's Fort was removed, and Schenectady once again had become an "open village."[102] However, John Henry and Bartholomew Clute, two pensioners, dispute this finding. They reported that Schenectady was surrounded with pickets. It had a fortress and other works which were guarded during the entire war, and that other works of defense were being constantly erected during the war. On June 23, 1780, an act was passed by the Legislature, enabling the inhabitants of Schenectady to erect a fortress, which was subsequently done.[103]

Richard Smith, who visited Schenectady in 1769, estimated the number of houses totaled 300. Regarding the use of bateaux, he reported:

> There are no wharves, but a public landing or two at the ends of the streets where bateaux bring the peltry and wheat from above. These bateaux are very large, each end sharp so that they may be rowed either way....The townspeople are supplied with beef and pork from New England, most of the meadows being used for wheat, peas, and other grain.[104]

Jabez Maud Fisher, the son of a wealthy Philadelphia ship owner, who traveled through Schenectady in 1773, placed the number of houses at 400; he also made special note of the "vast deal of fine meadow and arable ground in the neighborhood" and of the "very considerable and profitable trade carried on with the Indians." He further added: "There are several hundred boats that go from this place to Niagara, and some to Detroit loaded with dry and wet goods."[105]

Archaeological Documentation on the Teller Pasture

Several archaeological studies have been conducted on the Teller pasture, most involving studies for proposed sewer line projects. In October 1975, the New York State Office of Parks and Recreation, Division of Historic Preservation, conducted an archaeological reconnaissance study involving test pits along a proposed sewer line project in Rotunda Park (Riverside Park). Test pits 5 and 6 were located just east of North Street; test pit 7 was located 100 feet west of North Street on the former site of the William Schermerhorn parcel. All three of these test pits revealed considerable evidence of the presence of previous buildings, some of which could have been fill from demolition elsewhere. Test pit 5 contained a deep deposit of light brown sandy clay fill with much coal, coal ash and other debris, identified as being mostly from the nineteenth century. The maerial included both domestic refuse, as well as red brick chips, mortar and a blacksmith's hammer head 3 ¾ inches in length. At 34 inches, this deposit ended, revealing a light brown sandy clay alluvium. The vicinity around test pit seven was found to have been the most likely area for evidence of seventeenth or eighteenth century occupation, since material consistent with such a date appeared in the original alluvium layer. This area was not heavily-filled, and an early ground surface was present at twenty inches or twenty-five inches below the present grade. The early ground surface was described as "a fertile, dark brown sandy clay alluvium, which would be excellent for farming."[106]

Artifacts found include a single piece of frosted green-tinted window glass, a portion of a dark-green, hand-blown bottle dating to the eighteenth century or earlier, a shard of plain pearl ware (1785-1840), and a shard of black-glazed red earthenware (Jack field type), possibly from the 1760s to 1800. The testing did not reveal any evidence of prehistoric Indian occupation. The finding of early seventeenth or eighteenth century occupation on the William Schermerhorn parcel is consistent with a reference to "a dwelling house located on the northeast corner of my parcel near the Mohawk River," cited in William Schermerhorn's will.[107]

On October 17, 1995, workers, installing the North Street lateral water line, uncovered a contiguous row of thirteen rough timber posts aligned on a north-south axis, extending from 27 North Street three meters south to 25 North Street. The existence of this palisade line, lying parallel to North Street, could not be documented as belonging to any of the previously known stockade lines [108] An unpublished memo from Hartgen Archaeological Associates, related to the North Street lateral water line findings, reveals the following:

> A contiguous row of rough timber posts were found encapsulated in a narrow balk separating the new water line trench from an existing sewer line trench along the west side of North Street. Thirteen individual posts aligned on a north-south axis extended from 27 North Street three meters south to 25 North Street. All thirteen posts had been truncated approximately 60 centimeters below present street level. Archaeological excavation of the encapsulating soils indicates two nineteenth-century strata extending from 60 centimeters to 120 centimeters, overlying an eighteenth-century ground surface. The fact the posts were dug or driven into the eighteenth-century ground surface indicates the basis for our opinion that they were likely erected during the eighteenth century. The fact that they were erected hastily with little preparation, i.e., none were debarked, limbed or hewn, suggests their function was regarded as temporary.[109]

Figure 14. North Street Stockade Line. October 17, 1995. Courtesy of Maureen Gebert, Schenectady Heritage Area Coordinator.

Ceramics, such as fragments of stoneware and Chinese porcelain, that likely date from the time period (1740-1780) were found near the timbers. The fact that the ceramics were all manufactured and in use during the mid-late eighteenth century indicates the posts were erected at that time, according to Kevin Moody of Hartgen Archaeological Associates.

In June 1997, Hartgen Associates undertook *A Phase 1B Archaeological Investigation for the Schenectady Storm* Sewer *Expansion of Front Street.* A Trench 4 placement on the north side of Front Street about ten feet east of its intersection with North Street was chosen as a sampling of an area dating between the (ca. 1703) second stockade and the (ca. 1776) third stockade line and for the area's closeness to the Adam Vrooman House (ca. 1720) and the Johannes Teller House (ca. 1740).[110] This location had the potential to produce evidence of an early occupation, not directly related to the stockade structures. Surprisingly, excavation of the Trench 4 site produced no features or artifacts at all. Hartgen Associates reported the following:

> The lack of artifacts and features indicates the area was kept clean, an unusual tendency for Colonial period streets. Another possibility is that nineteenth century street surfacing, including grading, could have removed artifactual material that may have once been present.[111]

Archaeologists were confident they could find evidence of a third stockade line (ca. 1776). A Trench 5 location was chosen at the intersection of North College Street (Wall Street) where it intersected with Front Street. The third stockade is believed to have angled westerly from this location towards the foot of North Street. However, no evidence of the reputed 1776 stockade or of any earlier deposit relating to it was encountered.

> The lack of artifacts or stockade-related features from this area was surprising, given the reported proximity to the 1776 stockade line. Grading of the street areas may be responsible for removing the top of the buried topsoil and artifacts and features associated with it.[112]

Chapter Four - The 19th Century Teller Pasture

The Inland Lock Navigation Company would give rise to the Erie Canal (1817-1825). The construction of the Erie Canal through the central part of the city, together with the destructive fire of 1819, which completely destroyed the wharves, freighting establishments and storehouses, which lined the main *Binne Kil*, spelled the fate of the lower part of the city as a mercantile center. The development of Schenectady as a major railroad center would follow. George W. Featherstonaugh, a man of great scientific ability, became interested in the concept of steam railroads, and, starting in 1812, began to publish many articles on the subject. In 1826, he succeeded in securing the passage of a bill, incorporating the Mohawk and Hudson Railroad to run from Albany to Schenectady. A charter was granted soon thereafter. George W. Featherstonaugh and Stephen van Rensselaer, the Patroon, were the only directors named in the charter. In 1833, a charter was granted for the construction of the Utica and Schenectady Railroad; and, in 1843, the railroad running from Troy-Schenectady was completed. A series of personal tragedies caused Mr. Featherstonaugh to drift away from his railroad connections. In 1833, he became the first United States geologist. Others carried on the great enterprise he was so instrumental in starting. In 1848, the Schenectady Locomotive Engine Manufactory was established, and built its first locomotive, the "Lightning," the following year, just twenty years after George Stephenson's "Rocket," the first commercially successful steam locomotive had been invented. In 1851, the company was reorganized and renamed the Schenectady Locomotive Company. It would later merge with the American Locomotive Company.[113]

The Front and North Street Lots (1799-1816)

With the discovery of some previously unknown standardized assessment rolls for the City of Schenectady's First Ward, it is possible to document the ownership of the lots along Front and North Streets for the time period (1799-1803). The William Schermerhorn parcel, 57 Front Street (113 Front Street) can be used as a marker to trace the sequence of owners along Front Street, since the property was owner-occupied from 1744-1811. The house and lot at 59 Front Street (117 Front Street) was owned by William White for the entire time period (1799-1803).[114]

In 1799, 63 Front Street, the Adam Vrooman House, was still under the ownership of Volkje Veeder. By 1800, she shared the ownership with Engeltie (Angelica) van Vranken, her widowed sister. In 1802, Engeltie van Vranken became the sole owner of 63 Front Street, upon the death of Volkje Veeder.[115] This parcel remained under her ownership until her death in 1827, when her daughter, Harriet van Vranken, inherited it. Harriet van Vranken sold the Adam Vrooman House in 1852 to her cousins, Daniel McDougall, Nicholas van Vranken, and Daniel Barringer (Harriet Susan Vrooman). In 1853, her cousins deeded the property back to her.[116] Harriet van Vranken then sold the Adam Vrooman House to John I. Vedder, a blacksmith, reserving a life estate and the right to the use, occupancy and income from the property.[117] Mary Vedder, the widow of John I. Vedder, sold the parcel in 1858, upon the death of Harriet van Vranken, to Charles Whitmyer, a tailor and Prussian émigré. At the time of this sale, the lot dimensions (42 feet, 6 inches frontage, 114 feet, 2 inches, depth on the east side, and 38 feet, 6 inch along the rear of the parcel) remained the same as when Volekje Veeder had purchased the property in 1794.[118]

In 1799, 65 Front Street was still under the ownership of Jesse van Slyck, who had purchased the house lot in 1783 from the estate of John Sanders. Martin I. van Slyck, Jesse's son, owned the property briefly in 1800. In 1801, the property came into the possession of Cornelius van Vranken, who owned it until 1813. On November 28, 1801, Cornelius van Vranken married Rebecca Fonda Yates, the widow of Nicolas Yates. In 1803, Rebecca van Vranken is shown, in the sequence of names along Front Street, as the owner of land only.[119] It appears that Cornelius van Vranken's name may have inadvertently been omitted from the 1803 Assessment Roll, since he is later shown as the mortgagee of a deed, transferring the house lot at 65 Front Street, the Teller House, to Cornelius L. Barheydt, on May 7, 1813. At the time of this sale, the lot dimensions remained the same as when Jesse van Slyck had purchased the Teller House in 1783.[120]

Both 63 and 65 Front Street lots were originally surveyed as separate lots, and continue to remain so up to the present day. The easterly property line that changed on 63 Front Street after 1783 can be directly traced to the encroachment of Jesse van Slyck's lean-to brick addition, which angled four feet westerly onto Cornelius P. van Slyck's lot. The net effect of this change was to reduce the depth of the easterly property line of 63 Front Street from 118 feet to 114 feet, 2 inches. While this change was reflected in Volkje Veeder's deed of 1794, the change was never reflected in the deed for 65 Front Street. The westerly property line of the Teller House remained at 118 feet.[121]

Aaron Farnsworth, an early boat builder, is shown on the 1799 Assessment Roll as the owner of a house lot located at 67 Front Street (123 Front Street). This is the first documentation of a house appearing on the east side of North Street. The Assessment Roll of 1816 indicates that Aaron Farnsworth was still residing at 67 Front Street in 1816.[122]

Figure 15. 123-125-127 Front Street. Aaron Farnsworth House (on left). 1940. Courtesy of Efner Library.

The Assessment Roll of 1813 shows the following sequence of owners along Front Street: 57 Front Street: Counradt Ganswoord, a renter, "for the house and lot of Lawrence Schermerhorn," 59 Front Street: John van Petten; 63 Front Street: the widow, Angelica (Engeltie) van Vranken; 65 Front Street: Cornelius L. Barheydt; and

67 Front Street: Aaron Farnsworth.[123] John S. Glen is shown as an owner of land on North Street.

The 1816 Assessment Roll shows the following sequence of owners along Front Street: 57 Front Street: Henry Bastiaan "for the house and lot of Lawrence Schermerhorn," 59 Front Street: Jeremiah Fuller "for the house of Fuller next to the widow van Vranken residence," 63 Front Street: the widow Angelica (Engeltie) van Vranken; 65 Front Street: Cornelius L. Barheydt. Samuel Farnsworth is shown as the owner of a house and store on North Street.[124]

The Front and North Street Lots (1850-1900)

In 1850, *A Map of the City of Schenectady from an Accurate Survey*, published by M. Dripps, documents the presence of four houses located on the west side of North Street and five houses located on the east side of North Street. The Front Street houses numbered seven: four located on the west side of North Street, and three located on the east side. Outbuildings, such as sheds, barns and storehouses, although present, are not identified on this map; however, the Dutch burying ground is identified, encompassing the block from Green Street to Front Street. Its westerly property line is shown as being directly aligned with North Street.

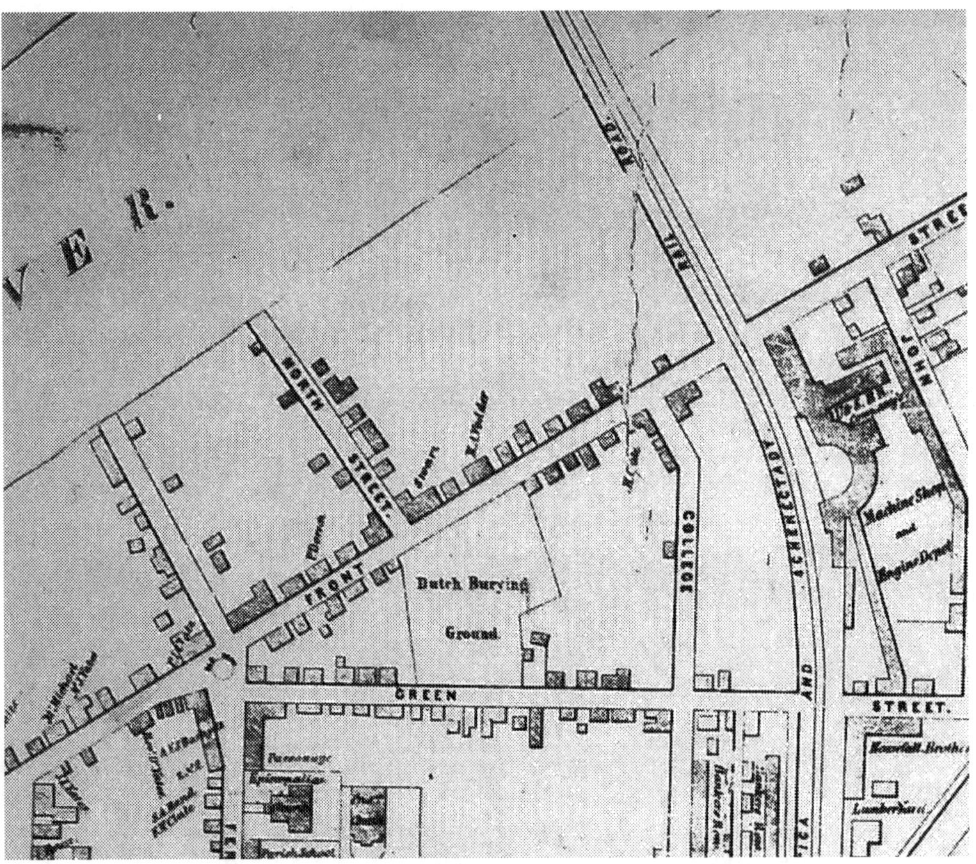

Figure 16. *Map of the City of Schenectady from an Accurate Survey*. 1850. M. Dripps, publisher. Courtesy of Schenectady Co. Historical Society.

Since there was a dearth of recorded deeds from ca. 1820 to 1850 and the last recorded deed of Daniel Vedder's (1877) makes no reference to a former owner of 65 Front Street, I began researching the Schenectady County Surrogate's Court for wills of the Vedder, Teller, or Glen families to see if the property had been devised by will. I discovered that Harmanus I. Vedder, Daniel Vedder's uncle, was the owner of record of the Teller House in the 1850s, and that the property had a barn (today's 5 North Street) and second dwelling house (today's 7 & 9 North Street) on it. Harmanus I. Vedder, born January 1786, was the eldest son of Johannes, son of Harmanus Albertse Vedder and Sarah Vedder, daughter of Nicolaas Vedder. Harmanus Albertse Vedder, his grandfather, married Susanna, daughter of Volkert Veeder, November 16, 1733. His great-grandfather was Albert Vedder, son of Harman Albertse Vedder, the first settler. His great-grandmother was Maria Glen, daughter of Johannes Sanders Glen, grand-daughter of Alexander Lindsay Glen.[125] Harmanus Vedder and Ann Guysling had no biological children, but were the adoptive parents of John S. Gow, born June 19, 1819, baptized March 14, 1824. His natural parents were Neal Gow and Mary Knowlton.[126] The New York State Census shows that Harmanus I. Vedder owned and occupied the Teller House in 1855. Harmanus I. Vedder made his will on September 1, 1853 and died on April 19, 1856. In his will, probated June 18, 1856, his wife Anna inherited the brick Teller House and had the use of the second house on the property, 30 North Street, during her lifetime. Upon her death, the first dwelling house and lot, the Teller House, as far as 9 inches from the southerly side of the barn, was devised to Harmanus I. Vedder's nephew, Daniel Vedder. The second house, including the barn, was devised to John S. Gow "who formerly resided with me." Anna M. Vedder died July 18, 1861.[127] On the 14th of August 1862, the second house and barn were transferred to Mary S. Gow, the widow of John S. Gow.[128]

> the dwelling house and lot on the corner of Front and North Lane, adjoining the lands of Harriet van Vranken, on which I now reside and also the dwelling house...lying north adjoining the above mentioned premises...for use during her natural life.[129]

Figure 17. Houses and Lot of Harmanus I. Vedder. 1850. The lot today (l.–r.): 121 Front Street, 5 North Street (John Gow's barn), and 7 & 9 North Street. C. Hamilton, photographer

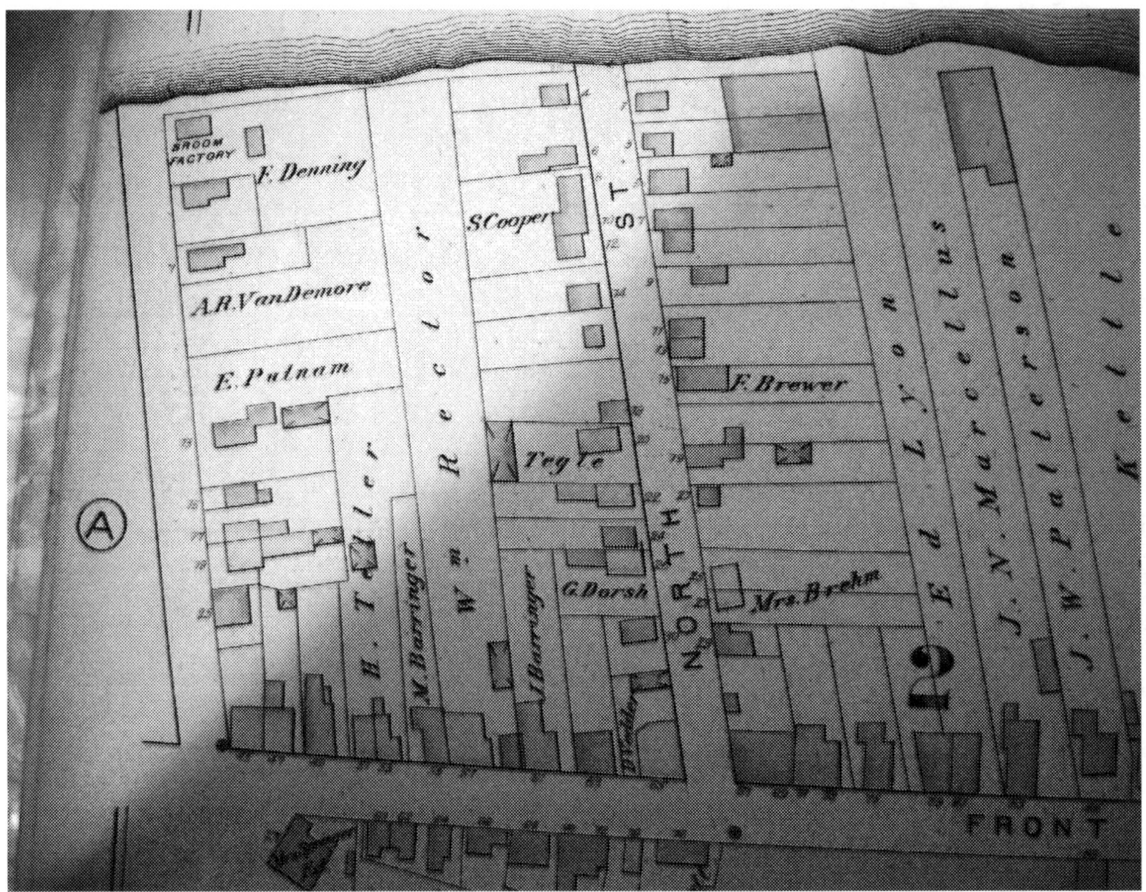

Figure 18. *The City Atlas of Schenectady, N.Y., 1880.* C. M. Hopkins, C.E., publisher. Courtesy of Schenectady Co. Historical Society.

On *The City Atlas of Schenectady, N.Y.*, published by C. M. Hopkins in 1880, the Teller House is identified as a large brick structure on 65 Front Street; the frame house is identified as belonging to 30 North Street, but John S. Gow's barn is still being shown as belonging to 65 Front Street, rather than as belonging to 30 North Street. Daniel Vedder is correctly identified on the map as the owner of 65 Front Street, the Teller House. *The City Atlas of Schenectady, N.Y. 1880* is consistent with *Plate 10 of the 1885 Assessment Roll of the City of Schenectady, Ward 2,* which identifies the lots along Front and North Streets. [130]

Daniel Vedder and Deborah, his wife, resided at 29 Front Street (32 Front Street after 1888). 65 Front Street (121 Front Street after 1888), the Teller House property, has historically been used as a boarding house. As far back as 1841, Simon Glen, a boat inspector and son of Col. John Glen, resided there. The Federal Census of 1860 shows that Herman Seaver, a teamster, his wife and son and Ahasuaris and Cornelia Mearcellis and their son boarded there. The City Directory of 1860 shows Thomas Osborne and his wife, both born in Ireland, and their two sons, who were laborers, residing at 65¼ Front Street (121¼ Front Street) and Andrew Van Buren, a boatman, his wife, a tailoress, and his mother-in-law, residing at 65½ Front Street (121½ Front Street).

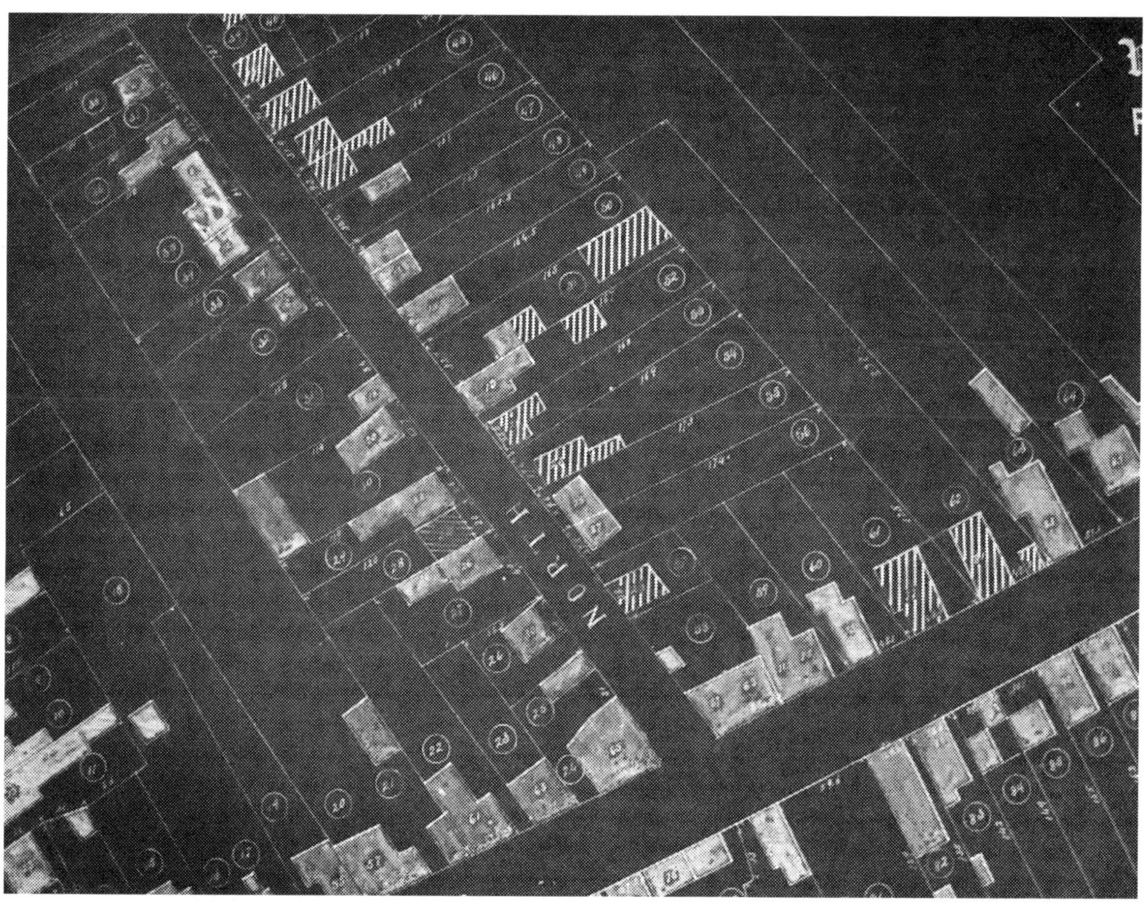

Figure 19. *Plate 10, 1885 Assessment Roll of the City of Schenectady, Ward 2.* Courtesy of Efner Library.

121½ Front Street (65½ Front Street) can be seen on *The Insurance Map of Schenectady, N.Y. October, 1889,* as a separate outbuilding on 121 Front Street (formerly 65 Front Street). In 1865, the New York State Census shows that the widow, Maria Gow and her seven children were still residing at 65 Front Street. She and her children continued to reside there until as late as 1870. Thomas Parker, a machinist born in England, his wife, and three children are also shown as residing at the Teller House in 1865.

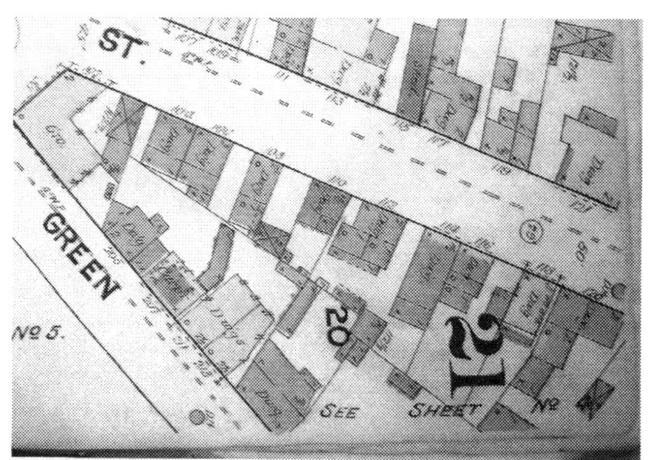

Figure 20. *Insurance Map of Schenectady, N.Y. October, 1889.* Sanborn-Perris Map Co. Courtesy of Schenectady Co. Historical Society.

On May 1, 1869, Daniel Vedder sold 65 Front Street to Thomas Pemberton, a locomotive engineer. Thomas Pemberton was the husband of Jane Vedder, Daniel Vedder's cousin.[131] Although the house was owner-occupied, boarders included: Thomas Williams, a blacksmith, born in England; John Howell, a boilermaker, born in England; Henry Larant, a car man, and his family; and William Mc Cumber, a laborer, his wife, and four children.[132] The Teller House would be re-possessed, sold at auction, and re-purchased by Daniel Vedder on December 12, 1877.[133] On April 12, 1877, Thomas L. Pemberton died in his 54th year; the funeral was held from his late residence, 65 Front Street.[134]

Figure 21. *Schenectady City, 1877.* Lucien Burleigh. Courtesy of Schenectady Co. Historical Society.

How could the Teller House accommodate all these boarders and families? Thanks to Lucien R. Burleigh of Troy, New York, a panoramic artist who walked each and every street sketching houses, trees, orchards, etc. to create his "bird's eye view" maps of northeastern New York, we have an accurate and complete depiction of the landscape of Schenectady in 1877. It is evident from *Schenectady City: 1877* that the Teller House had a full-sized framed, lean-to addition annexed onto an existing brick lean-to addition. Also, Harmanus I. Vedder was renting the frame house to Mrs. Baumaghim prior to his death in 1856. Although the barn and second house were inherited by Mary S. Gow as of August 1862, she continued to reside with her in-laws in the Teller House and rented out both John Gow's barn (as a residence) and the frame house (30 North Street). She did not sell the barn and frame house until March 1, 1881. The lot dimensions at the time of the sale were: 53 feet frontage on North Street by 41 feet depth on North Street.[135]

In 1880, the Teller House would be rented to two families: Frederick Fagle, a broom maker from Prussia, his wife and three children; and Edward D. Rouse, a boilermaker from England, his wife, daughter and widowed aunt. Edward D. Rouse and his family lived at 65 Front Street through 1887. Henry Springer, a laborer, is shown as a boarder from 1881 to 1885. In 1888, the street numbers in the city changed. 65 Front Street became 121 Front Street; and 30 North Street became 7 and 9 North Street. In 1888, Edward D. Rouse moved to 123 Front Street (formerly 67 Front Street).[136]

On August 9, 1882, Daniel Vedder died. At the time of his death, he had been the oldest-tenured dry goods merchant in the city, starting in 1844 as a clerk in the store of Cornelius S. Groot and Sons.[137] In his will, he left his wife, Deborah, the right to all the rents and income, to be paid to her semi-annually during her lifetime. If the sums proved to be insufficient, the executors were directed to take monies out of the principal of the estate. When Emmett O'Neil, one of the executors named, renounced his rights to letters testamentary, and, upon probate of the estate, Deborah Vedder remained as sole executrix until her death, with full power of sale. Daniel Vedder, a philanthropist, had established a $5,000.00 scholarship fund in his name for an indigent student at Union College and a $400.00 award for the best declamation in the Classical Department. Having tragically lost his son, Frank, and daughter, Anna, both at the age of 14, it was his intent that John Vedder, Charles E. Scott, William Vedder, and Nicholas Scott, the nephews of his deceased brother and sister, inherit from his estate. Upon the death of his wife, the Teller House and the remainder of Vedder's residual estate were to be bequeathed to The Home of the Friendless, a benevolent organization that provided housing for destitute and homeless women.[138]

After the death of Daniel Vedder, Deborah Vedder continued to reside at her primary residence, 29 Front Street. The Federal Census of 1900 shows that 121 Front Street continued to be rented to two families: E. C. Becker, a paperhanger, his wife and three children; and to Arthur Mc Cassey, a machinist, his wife and three children. Ernest Mc Cassey, a steamfitter, also boarded there. The former barn of John S. Gow is finally separately identified as 5 North Street and is shown as the residence of Alfred Yauchter, a watchmaker, his wife and two children.[139] 7 and 9 North Street, now a duplex, is shown as being rented by two families: Agnts Syndwoldt, a machinist from Germany, his wife and three sons; and Charles Fry, a day laborer, his wife and three children.[140] The 1902 New York State Census shows that Martin Schenck, a machinist, his wife and two children, were renting 121 Front Street.[141]

Deborah Vedder died April 8, 1909. The Teller House was transferred to the Old Ladies Home (Home of the Friendless) on April 7, 1909, one day before Deborah Vedder's death. The Home of the Friendless never became a recipient of Daniel Vedder's residual estate.[142]

Chapter Five – The 20th Century Teller Pasture

The outstanding Mohawk Valley features that marked the twentieth century were the growth and development of the electrical industry, the establishment of hydro-electric power plants and artificial reservoir systems and the expansion of river and land transportation systems. The rise of the automobile and a system of automobile highways overshadowed the growth of the other transportation systems, namely, developments in the New York Central Railroad and electric trolley lines and the construction of the New York State Barge Canal (1905-1918).[143]

The twentieth century marked "the changing of the guard" on the Teller pasture. With the passing of Harriet van Vranken and John I. Vedder, the legacy of 63 Front Street (119 Front Street), the Adam Vrooman House, had passed out of the hands of the many generations of Tellers, Vedders, Veeders, van Slycks, and van Vrankens, who had resided there. The legacy now belonged to Charles Whitmyer, a tailor, and Prussian émigré.[144]

The legacy of 65 Front Street (121 Front Street), the Teller House, would suffer a similar fate, with the passing of Harmanus I. Vedder in 1856, the sudden death of John S. Gow, his adopted son, and the death in 1882 of Daniel Vedder, Harmanus I. Vedder's nephew. It appears that the Teller House, which had housed the descendants of Willem Teller, and the skilled artisans who worked in the boat-building industry during the critical period of the French and Indian War, the Revolutionary War, and the War of 1812 was losing its identity with its past. When the Teller House was transferred to the Old Ladies Home (Home of the Friendless) on April 7, 1909, it marked the first time in the 245 year history of the pasture that a Teller descendant, or an in-law of a Teller descendant, had not owned the property.[145] It is not known whether the Old Ladies Home used the property as an adjunct home to house "inmates," or whether the rentals alone served as a source of revenue

Figure 22. Home of the Friendless, 237 Green Street (ca. 1905). Courtesy of Efner Library

to support the newly-constructed three-story home at 1519 Union Street, today's Heritage Home for Women. The cost for this home had escalated from an estimated $28,000.00 to $33,000.00.[146] It had been rumored that bed-ridden patients were being housed in overcrowded conditions in the dining room of the Teller House, their beds separated only by sheets hung from a tin ceiling. Boarders included the Hallowell family--Elizabeth, a teacher, and her retired siblings--Margaret G. and Robert Hallowell; and Margaret Keeler, a domestic employed by the Home. Margaret Keeler later served as the matron of the Old Ladies Home (Home of the Friendless) from April 1919 to June 1921.[147] Charles Judeman, a public hall janitor, born in Germany, his wife and two children were also residing at the house.

On May 5, 1910, Margaret G. Hallowell purchased the property from the Old Ladies Home. The lot dimensions measured 39.75 feet frontage, 68 feet, 5 inches along North Street, 41 feet 5 inches on the northerly side, and 59 feet on the westerly side. This marked a change from the previous property dimensions of 66 feet, 5 inches along North Street, and of 42 feet, 9 inches across the rear of the parcel. When Margaret Hallowell died on September 25, 1911, her sister, Elizabeth Hallowell, inherited the Teller House.[148]

Elizabeth Hallowell continued to live in the Teller House until her death in 1918, when the property was sold, by her heirs to George and Nettie Keeler on April 17, 1918.[149] Margaret S. Keeler, sister of George Keeler and matron of the Old Ladies Home, and Albert Springer, an assembler at General Electric, continued to board at the Teller House for several years.[150]

George and Nettie Keeler lived their entire lives in the Teller House. George Keeler died August 17, 1934; his wife died intestate June 27, 1946. Their only son, John S. Keeler, died intestate on December 1, 1974. His only son, John Francis Keeler, deeded his interest to his widowed mother, Frances H. Keeler, on December 6, 1974.[151] The deed was officially recorded on April 16, 1975, the same day the Teller House was sold to Axel R. Frieberg.[152]

The Teller House Restoration (1976-1979)

On four separate occasions over a span of twenty years, Axel and Mildred Frieberg had planned on a Teller House closing, only to be informed by Francis H. and John S. Keeler that they had changed their minds. By the time Francis H. Keeler, the widow of John S. Keeler, contacted Axel Frieberg to again discuss the sale of the property, the exterior brick walls of the Teller House were crumbling, the roof needed replacing, the plaster walls were collapsing and the sills were rotting. In short, the house was uninhabitable. Axel Frieberg, now a widower, was reluctant at first to purchase the property, but abruptly changed his mind. In memory of his wife, he decided to spare no expense in making his (and his wife's) dream, of restoring the eighteenth century rural Dutch Colonial home, become a reality.

Figure 23. Rear View of the Teller House. 1976. Courtesy of Edward Gifford

Since the Teller House had been under the ownership of the Keeler family for a period of 57 years, I was hopeful that Edward Gifford, close personal friend and the executor of Axel

Frieberg's estate, could provide some insight into the pristine (original) condition of the house prior to its restoration. Edward Gifford recalled that Axel Frieberg had purchased a house devoid of its entire contents and in deplorable condition. The built-in cabinets and cupboards, the Delft tiles surrounding the fireplaces and many of the original Dutch doors had been removed, most likely for their salvage value.

The brick exterior walls on the southeast corner of the house had separated to such a degree that light was emanating through them. No furnishings were to be found anywhere. Sometime prior to my interview with Edward Gifford, I had had the opportunity to speak with Danny Blythe, who, as a youth, had been hired by Doug Cater, an auctioneer, to salvage the contents of the Teller House. He vividly recalled how he and Doug Cater removed a large wooden sign, carved in the shape of a fish, from the house. He remembered it was painted orange and had the word "fish" carved into it. Danny Blythe described the sign as being several feet in length, oval in shape, fully 3-dimensional, and hewn out a huge log. The fish had a triangular-shaped tail and its scales had been elaborately carved. He described it as a "folk art trade sign" that would rest outside of a building. The sign was not hinged in any respect. When I later questioned Edward Gifford as to whether he had ever seen the "folk art trade sign," his response was an emphatic: "No, I would have definitely remembered it."[153]

Figure 24. Southeast Corner of the Teller House. 1976. Courtesy of Edward Gifford.

Danny Blythe described the house as "needing a lot of work" and thought the house was in the process of being renovated. He recalled he had removed two matching built-in corner cupboards from the dining room. He could not remember the exact year he had been there, but thought maybe it was ca.1980.

Edward Sutton, the chief carpenter of the Teller House restoration, recalled there had been two bedrooms located on the second floor. These bedrooms were further partitioned into two by boards, which were covered by newspapers and other materials, to make the rooms appear more attractive. There had been a walk-in closet located between the bedrooms, but this was eliminated during the restoration to create two private bathrooms. Two wooden toilets were found; the sole bathroom was located somewhere in the kitchen area. The original windows were framed with six inch square beams and were pegged together. These, Axel Frieberg believed, had been taken from the original Dutch house because the beams were scorched. The roof boards showed signs of scorching, as well.[154]

The architect's plan had called for three Dutch-styled dormers to be built on the front of the house, but the Stockade Association had ruled that if dormers were to be built, they had to be gabled (English-style). Therefore, the decision was made not to construct any dormers on the front façade at all. Ironically, when the shingles were removed, there was evidence that two Dutch-style dormers had been in place previously, and that a roof had projected out over the front steps, similar to the architectural plan. The planks were still in evidence.[155]

All the floors and ceilings were found to be original to the house. The beams in the garret room (east bedroom), including the hand-wrought nails and hooks, were all original as well. They were uncovered during the process of removing an early pressed-board ceiling.

The cellar door in the downstairs hallway was original to the house as were the closet and bathroom doors. The entry door to both bedrooms and to the second floor hallway closet were replicated from the design of the cellar door.[156]

Figure 25. Original Cellar Door. Teller House. 1979. Courtesy of Edward Gifford.

An original window sash, found in the cellar, showed the configuration of the panes, 12 over 8 on the main floor, 6 over 6 on the second floor. This was used as a template to replicate all the window sashes. The old sills, which were made from a single block of wood, had rotted. They were replaced in the same fashion as the original sills--using a single block of wood. The lintel over the front door had to be replaced, including the fan made to hold the bricks from sagging onto the frame.[157]

Figure 26. Lintels and Sills, partially restored (ca. 1976). Courtesy of Edward Gifford.

The fireplaces were barely recognizable prior to the restoration. Tile flues had to be installed in the fireplaces to bring them up to code. The Delft tiles on the living and dining room fireplaces had been removed, as had the Federal-style mantel in the living room. Axel Frieberg was able to purchase a batch of authentic mid-eighteenth century Dutch tin-glazed tiles, which had been salvaged from a Dutch house in the area. When the fireplace surrounds were completed, he still lacked two tiles. He was later able to purchase several tin-glazed tiles of the same pattern (a basket of flowers within a cartouche, with Wan-Li corners) from an antique store in Rockport, Massachusetts. These replacement tin-glazed tiles would later prove not to be original to the eighteenth century.[158]

Figure 27. Federal Fireplace, Teller House. 1976. Courtesy of Edward Gifford.

The exterior brick had to be power-washed and any deteriorating or missing bricks had to be replaced before pointing work could begin. The water-struck bricks, which separate the wall from the foundation, had to be specially-made. The mortar used had to be mixed with special sand to simulate the original brick color. The sand was obtained from Schalren's pit, located on Middle line Road. A beehive oven had to be totally rebuilt.

Since current building codes prevent the replacement of a wood-shingled roof, the rafters were reinforced to support the weight of a slate roof. The original clapboard siding on the west end of the house had been taken off and replaced with an artificial brick siding. This was replaced with an authentic copy of the original weather boards. Hoddy van Voast had the "proper" plane to hand-cut each board.[159]

Figure 28. Federal Fireplace, Teller House, partially restored. 1976. Courtesy of Edward Gifford.

Figure 29. Pre-Restoration Brick Work for Beehive Oven. Courtesy of Edward Gifford.

The interior walls and floors were cracked, and plaster was falling down. The floor boards had to be shored up. The center hall stairway was collapsing, as well. The treads overshooting the risers were copied from the existing staircase. An original spindle, found in the cellar, served as a template for the restoration of the banister.

Figure 30. Pre-Restoration of Center Hall Stairway and Walls. 1976. Courtesy of Edward Gifford.

Edward Gifford and Edward Sutton recalled that a pintel, found in the basement, led them to believe that a split Dutch door led into the center hallway. The split Dutch door and the line of six bulls-eye glass sections over the door were copied from Fort Crailo. Axel Frieberg was able to purchase the six bull's-eye glass sections in England.

Axel Frieberg had taken out a second mortgage (generously provided by Edward Gifford) and had spent all of his life savings, including an inheritance, to restore the Teller House. Edward Gifford estimated that the total monies spent exceeded $90,000.00 over a span of three years. Axel Frieberg died on August 18, 1993. Only one offer was made on the house, by Paul Mulligan for $215,000.00 including the furnishings. This offer was refused. Edward Gifford sold the house on August 2, 1995 for $140,000.00 to Richard W. and Linda Wegener. The furnishings were sold separately in an estate sale for $50,000.00.[160]

After owning the Teller House for just four years, the Wegeners sold the property on April 5, 1999 to Gregory D. Harper and Josephine Sorenson, joint tenants with the right of survivorship.[161] Josephine Sorenson conveyed her interest in the house to Gregory D. Harper on October 26, 2001.[162]

Chapter Six – The 21st Century Teller Pasture

As the twenty-first century began, the Teller House would once again be sold. On May 7, 2002, the property was transferred to Anthony Sassi, an antique collector and dealer, and his wife, Marilyn Sassi, a museum curator.[163] They, too, had dreamed of owning the eighteenth century rural Dutch Colonial Teller House. Regrettably, Anthony Sassi died in 2004, but his (and his wife's) dream would live on. Marilyn Sassi would never allow the legacy of the Teller House to die.

Archaeological Rescue/Salvage Project of 121 Front Street (October, 2002)

In the fall of 2002, Anthony and Marilyn Sassi contracted with Donovan Restoration to modify their backyard landscaping to include expansion of the existing carport, the construction of a stone retaining wall and walkway, and the planting of a shrub bed.

In October 2002, Anthony and Marilyn Sassi gave Ronald Kingsley of the Schenectady County Community College's Community Archaeology Program (SCCC-CAP) permission to conduct a rescue/ salvage study on the site before construction work began.[164] The archaeological investigation centered upon four areas of study: the back door entry way, the carport embankment retaining wall and terrace, shovel testing on the yard terrace and backhoe stripping by the contractor to expose the terrace soil. Selected areas were examined to a maximum depth of two feet.

Two layers of soil (A & B) were found to be present within the generally flat surface of the backyard. The upper (A) layer was found to be shallower, 6 inches in depth, closer to the house, increasing to 12 inches in depth towards the rear of the yard. This finding suggested that the earlier (deeper) surface (B) declined northerly towards the river. The upper (A) layer was interpreted as a fill deposit. Possible sources of this fill could include soil from the excavated cellar, re-deposited soil from the digging of the first carport and/or fill from a more distant site.

Shovel testing verified the changes in the depth of the (A) layer at ST 1 and ST 2. A brick pillar footing from a nineteenth century structure was exposed at the interface between the two soil layers (A & B) at ST 1. A search for such a structure or outbuilding might be found on panoramic maps of the late nineteenth century, or, possibly, on insurance maps of the city. Indications of additional structures and outbuildings on the Teller House parcel are discernible on *Schenectady*

City: 1877, a panoramic map published by the H. H. Bailey Company; however, the views, at ground level, are partially obscured. Oakley H. Bailey and his brother published panoramic maps from 1874 to as late as 1927, first under the name of "bird's eye views" and later as "aero views." In an interview in 1932, Oakley H. Bailey noted: "The business has been practically without competition, as so few can give it the patience, care and skill essential for its success, but now the airplane cameras are covering the territory and can put more towns on paper in a day than was possible in months by hand work formerly." Insurance maps of the City of Schenectady have proven valuable in showing changes occurring to streets, main residence and some outbuildings, such as barns, over time. However, these maps do not necessarily identify smaller structures, such as porches or smaller sheds. In addition, these maps show inconsistencies between map companies (and sometimes within the same company) over a period of years.

Figure 31. *Schenectady City: 1875.* H. H. Bailey & Co. Courtesy of Schenectady Co. Historical Society.

Artifacts found within the deeper (B) layer reflected a time range from the mid-eighteenth to mid-nineteenth century. Artifacts found in the upper (A) layer reflected a narrower and more recent time, ranging from the nineteenth to early twentieth century. A collection of buttons, found on the west side of the back door entry, may have been associated with tailoring activities on the property.

Archaeological Study of 29 North Street (September, 2008)

The foundation of a former building was discovered when Reverend Dennis Meyer, the owner of 29 North Street, was having a utility trench dug along the river side of his lot. The trench exposed a section of non-mortared greywacke stone (commonly used for foundations during the eighteenth and nineteenth centuries) and a large deposit of cinders, ash and anthracite coal at the rear of the site. Material finds include a soft orange brick (used as a wall filler during the eighteenth and nineteenth centuries), some fragments of hard red brick (used for exposed areas), a section of a colorless glass bottle, a piece of thick sheet window glass, a piece of milk glass, two hand-forged wrought iron nails (a "T" and a "rose" head), a section of a stoneware crock, a shard of white ware, and a shard of blue-design transfer print earthenware. The archaeological finds suggest that the portion of the building uncovered was constructed sometime around the mid-1800s and was occupied into the 1900s.[165]

It is difficult to trace the origins of the discovered foundation, since the riverfront's shoreline has changed so dramatically over the years. Today's North Street is approximately 614 feet in length. Riverside Park accounts for 200 feet of this. This distance has remained relatively constant since 1894.

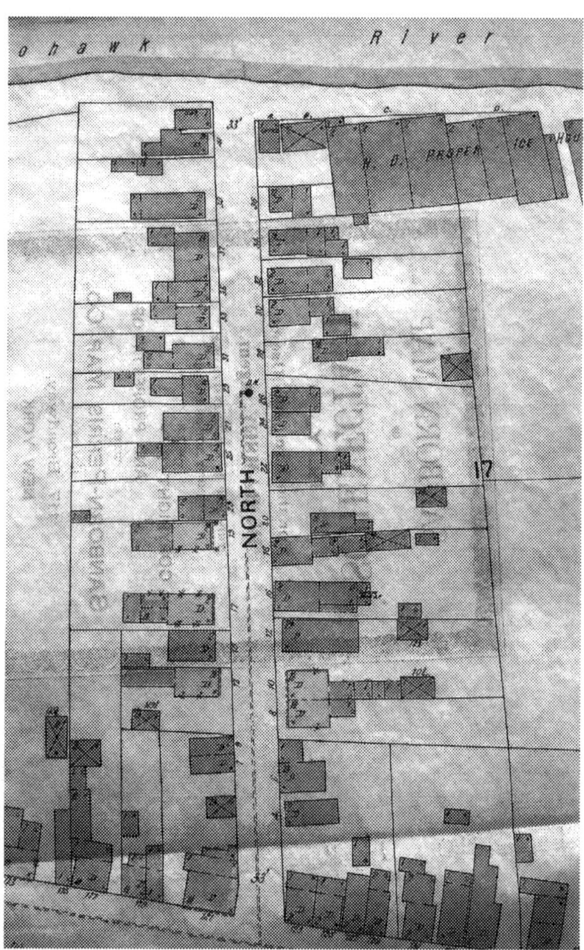

Figure 32. *Insurance Map of the City of Schenectady, N.Y. 1894*. Sanborn-Perris Map Co., publishers. Courtesy of Schenectady Co. Historical Society.

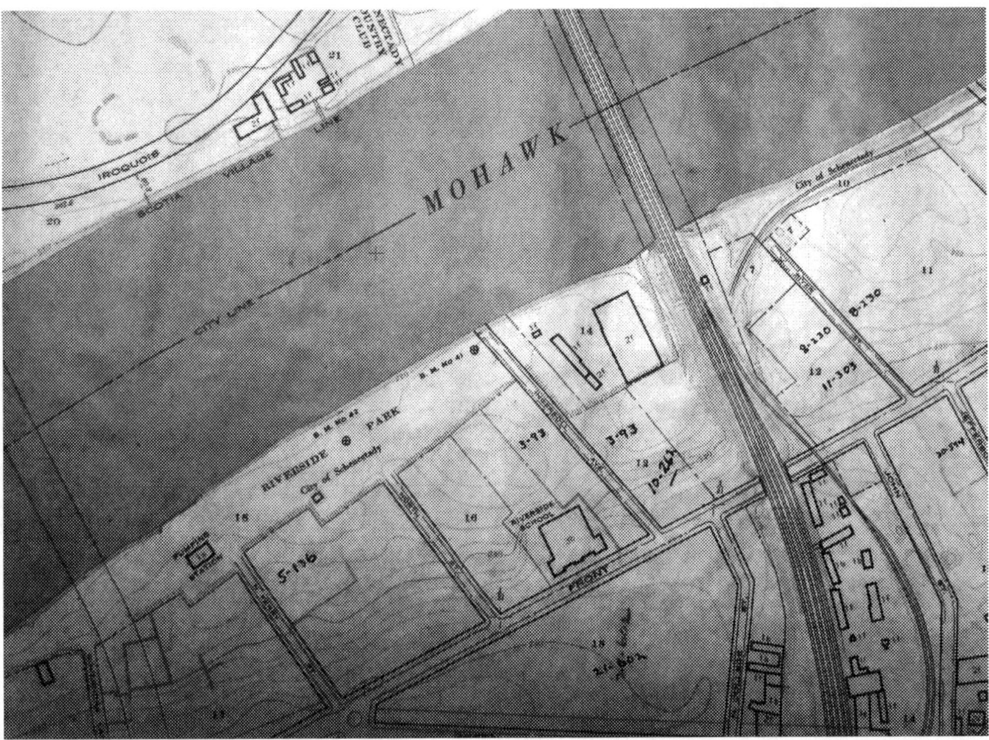

Figure 33. *City of Schenectady Geodetic and Topographical Survey, Sheet 11. 1928.* Randall Map Co.

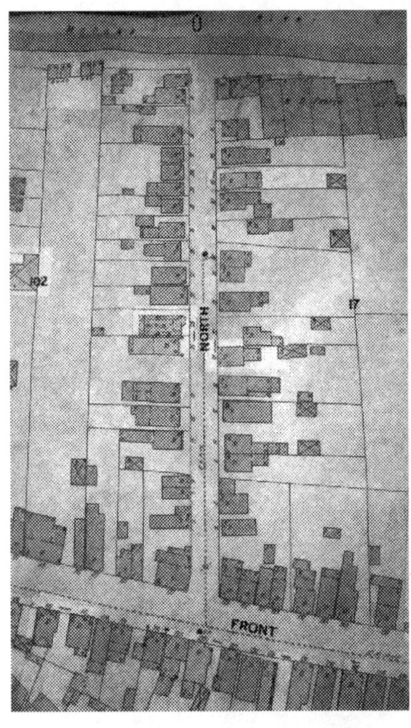

Figure 34. *Insurance Map of the City of Schenectady, N.Y. 1900* (Revised to 1912). Sanborn Map Company. Courtesy of the Efner Library.

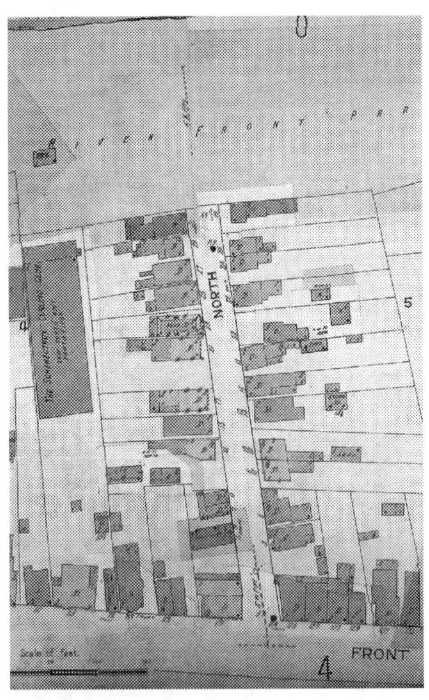

Figure 35. *Insurance Map of the City of Schenectady, N.Y. 1914* (Revised to 1929). Sanborn Map Company. Courtesy of the Efner Library.

The Insurance Map of the City of Schenectady, N.Y. 1900 (Revised to 1912) shows North Street prior to the construction of Riverside Park. There were no apparent changes to the Front Street lots during this time span. 29 and 31 North Street, the site of the recently discovered foundation, appears on the *Insurance Map of the City of Schenectady, N.Y. 1900 (Revised to 1912).* 25 to 27 North Street (the site of the North Street stockade line) appear on this map as well. Note the location of these sites in relation to the Mohawk River.

The Insurance Map of the City of Schenectady, N.Y. 1914 (Revised to 1929) shows that Riverside Park (Riverfront Park) has replaced street numbers 33 to 41 on North Street. Note the location of 29 and 31 North Street (the site of the recently discovered foundation) and of 25 to 27 North Street (the site of the North Street stockade line) in relation to Riverside Park and the Mohawk River. *The Insurance Map of the City of Schenectady, N.Y. 1914* also shows that changes have been made to 5 North Street between 1914 and 1929.

Summary and Interpretative Findings

The Teller pasture, a five-acre plat of ground granted to Willem Teller as part of the Schenectady Patent of 1664, quickly evolved from its original purpose as a pasture supporting the agricultural needs of the village of Schenectady and of the Dutch Province. On August 27, 1664, shortly after the founding of Schenectady, the Province came under English rule. Schenectady would suffer the effects of the first of four French and Indian Wars in 1690, when the village was burned to the ground–a victim of King William's War (1689-1697). This war and each of three successive French and Indian Wars inevitably impacted the evolution of the Teller pasture. Just twelve years later, Queen Anne's War (1702-1713) was declared. Queen Anne's Fort was ordered built on the site of the destroyed Fort Dongan. The construction of the Fort marked the expansion of the first stockade line north to the banks of the Mohawk River, and to the re-routing and expansion of Front Street to the north and east of the Queen Anne's Fort. The pasture's purpose changed dramatically around 1740, when war and the imminent threats of war necessitated the creation of a road accessible to the boatyards of the "Strand Street/River" and to the docks on the Mohawk River for the transport of goods and military ordinance. The Teller pasture (North Street) became the designated site for such a road. As the threat of a third conflict neared, King George's War (1744-1748), the people of the pasture began mobilizing for war.

It appears that the division of lands had begun just prior to the death of Johannes Teller in 1744. Joseph C. Yates, a blacksmith, came into possession of the entire easterly-third of the pasture by 1759. He was already in possession of a parcel on the west side of North Lane, well prior to Johannes Teller's death. Joseph C. Yates transferred his riverbank parcel to his son-in-law, Cornelius Peek, a wheelwright, and sold the abutting parcel near the Mohawk River to his father-in-law, Jellis Fonda, a carpenter. Abraham Fonda came into possession of the riverbank parcel, west of North Street, as early as 1754.

The boat-building families--the van Slycks, Veeders, Marselises, and van Epses worked on the "Strand Street/River" at the end of North Lane, the site for the construction and the staging of hundreds of bateaux attached to military expeditions during King George's War (1744-1748), the French and Indian War (1755-1763), and the Revolutionary War (1775-1783). It appears that the Front Street houses (59 Front Street, 63 Front Street, and 65 Front Street) all served as shelter to the boat builders and to the support personnel who worked on the "Strand Street/River." On April 13, 1754, North Street was cut through for the hauling of timber to the riverbank. The fourth and final French and Indian War (1755-1763) began the following year.

The discovery of the only known mid-eighteenth century surveyed map, showing the palisades of the village of Schenectady, *A Geographical Plan of Schenectady*, September 9, 1756, drawn by Captain Gustav C. Wetterstrom, a British military engineer, clearly identifies the location of the second stockade, its gates, and its fortifications at the time of the French and Indian War (1755-1763). It is consistent with an earlier unsurveyed map, *A Plan of Schenectady,* drawn from the memory of a British soldier. This map's date, accuracy, and reliability had often been questioned.

The critical role North Street played in the French and Indian War (1755-1763) was brought to the forefront when a contiguous row of thirteen timbers, comprising a North Street stockade line, was unearthed on October 17, 1995. Archaeologists determined that this stockade line dated to the mid-eighteenth century. This discovery raised the question of whether this previously undocumented stockade line could have been part of a third stockade. Attempts made to discover the easternmost line of the third stockade, which reputedly angled westerly from College Street to the foot of North Street, continues to prove unsuccessful to date.

The parcels on the Teller pasture passed down through the blood lines of Willem Teller and Alexander Lindsay Glen, whose familial and business ties date back to Holland and to the West India Company ("GWC"). Their first alliances in the Indian trade, with Jacques Corneliese van Slyck and Harmen Vedder would prove to be extremely strong. Soon, they would all be bonded by blood and circumstance. Their generational hold on the pasture would continue well into the nineteenth century.

As the mid-nineteenth century neared, an influx of immigrants from England, Prussia, Germany, and Ireland appeared on the pasture and made it their home. They found employment mainly as canal workers or as locomotive engineers, machinists, steamfitters, and laborers in the railroad industry.

The origin of the Front Street houses was explored in depth. The mystery of who built the red, brick, gambrel-roofed Teller House remains unanswered; however, there is no evidence to date that links Jesse van Slyck to the Teller House prior to 1783. The last known owner of the Teller House prior to 1783 was John Sanders. In all likelihood, he owned the Teller House in 1765 when John S. Glen sold his father's (Abraham Glen's) interests in the Glen estate to Deborah Glen.[166] Our best clue to the ownership of the Teller House probably comes from Willem Teller himself. He was emphatic in demanding that the lands bestowed to Johannes Teller:

> Shall devolve upon the children of Johannes Teller, to be made over to the son or sons, with such compensation or satisfaction to the daughters as he in conscience shall find to be proper.[167]

Whether Johannes, son of Johannes, who died unmarried in 1744, deeded the Front Street *lots* to his two surviving sisters, Maria (Teller) Glen and Annatje (Teller) Vedder is unknown, but is highly probable. The 1782 mortgage deed, John Cuyler to Cornelius P. van Slyke, does appear to link Annatje (Teller) Vedder to the Adam Vrooman House. John Cuyler, Annatje Vedder's son-in-law, sold the parcel just prior to the death of Susanna Vedder. Why 63 Front Street was known as the Adam Vrooman House remains a mystery, since the house is located well within the parameters of the Teller pasture. Adam Vrooman and his sons were carpenters, so one of them may have built the house. However, no deed has come to light that shows the transfer of either the house or lot to Adam Vrooman, or to one of his sons.

Lastly, the evolvement of the signature Teller House was explored in depth. An examination of the walls and foundations of the house reveal that the hybrid Georgian house, built ca. 1760, had an earlier Dutch history contained within it. The framework of the center hallway and easterly wing were constructed during the early decades of the eighteenth century. While the house initially appeared mainly Georgian in concept, several of its early Dutch features, including the "weather boarded" west gable end and the steeply-pitched Dutch staircase, with its high risers and overhanging treads, were retained. We were given an unprecedented glimpse into the Teller House restoration (1976-1979) through the photo-journaling efforts of Edward Gifford and the late Axel Frieberg. Ironically, the rural Dutch Colonial house, owned by the wealthiest of the wealthiest of Dutch patricians, would suffer from the hardest of times and fall into the hands of those least able to maintain it. Daniel Vedder, who had initially sold the Teller House to Thomas Pemberton, a Vedder/Teller relative, would see his house re-possessed and sold at auction. Daniel Vedder would re-purchase the signature Teller House shortly before his death– the house which had served as home to the myriad number of Teller relatives and to the boat-building families who worked on the "Strand Street/River." In the second half of the nineteenth century and early twentieth century, the house would serve as home to a considerable number of first-generation English, German, Irish, and Prussian immigrants. With the demise of Deborah Vedder in 1909, the Teller House would be donated to the Home of the Friendless, a benevolent organization that provided housing for destitute and homeless women. The house then became home, first to the Hallowell family, secondly to the Keeler family, who had been long-time boarders at the Teller House. In retrospect, the three generations of the Keeler family, who owned the house for fifty-seven years, inadvertently, can be credited with leaving the house in its pristine (original) state. They could ill afford to modify the Teller House to adapt to the conventions and styles of later times. However, the darker side of this was that the Teller House fell into a state of total disrepair, only to be saved from total collapse by the late Axel Frieberg, a lover of all things old, who dedicated his remaining years to restoring the Teller House to its ca. 1760s glory.

Endnotes

1. Arnold J. F. Van Laer, "Translations of the Letter from Arent van Curler to Kilaen van Rensselaer." *Dutch Settlers Society of Albany Yearbook 2* (1926-1927).
2. Daniel K. Richter, *The Ordeal of the Longhouse: The Peoples of the Iroquois League in the Era of European Colonization*. Chapel Hill: University of North Carolina Press, 1992.
3. Charles T. Gehring, "Light on New Netherlands." Translated by Charles T. Gehring, Albany: New York State Museum Exhibit, December, 2008.
4. James W. Bradley, *Before Albany: An Archaeology of Native-Dutch Relations in the Capital Region: 1660-1664*. New York: University of the State of New York, 2007. The Proto-Historic period is defined by James Bradley as the period when European materials had reached Native people, but before Europeans came inland. For background information on the Mohican people, reference Shirley W. Dunn, *Mohicans and Their Land, 1609-1730*. Fleischmann's, N.Y.: Purple Mountain Press.
5. Ibid. 37.
6. Gehring, "Light on New Netherlands."
7. Ibid.
8. Gehring, "Light on New Netherlands." Robert Juet, the English first mate, printed the only surviving account in English, in 1625.
9. Bradley, BA, 37. The Independent Traders Period, as designated by J. Bradley, is based on the type of glass beads found on Mohican and Mohawk sites diagnostic of the period 1609-1624, when the Carel-Soop Glass House in Amsterdam, Holland was identified as the producer and exporter of these beads. It is also defined as the date when Henry Hudson sailed up the Hudson River in search of a Northeast Passage, but before the West India Company was chartered in 1621.
10. Gehring, "Light on New Netherlands: West India Company." The location of Fort Nassau on Castle Island has never been found.
11. Gehring, "Light on New Netherlands: Dutch Atlantic World".
12. Ibid.
13. Arnold J. F. Van Laer, ed. and trans. *Van Rensselaer Bowier Manuscripts,* Albany: University of the State of New York, 1908. 166-169.
14. Russell Shorto, *Island at the Center of the World: The Epic Story of Dutch Manhattan and the Forgotten Colony That Shaped America*. New York: Doubleday, 2004.
15. Van Laer, "Translations of the Letter from Arent van Curler to Kilaen van Rensselaer."

16. Gehring, "Light on New Netherlands: Fort Nassau, Fort Orange and Beverwijck." Reference: Janny Venema, *Beverwijck: A Dutch Village on the American Frontier, 1652-1664.* Albany: State University of New York Press, 2003.
17. Thomas E. Burke, *Mohawk Frontier: The Dutch Community of Schenectady, New York, 1661-1710.* Ithaca and London: Cornell University Press, 1991. 10.
18. Ibid. 38. The surveying procedure was a formal one. Governor Peter Stuyvesant would order the inhabitants "to have their cultivated and uncultivated land surveyed by the sworn surveyor (Jacques Cortelyou)...also, to have it marked and divided by the proper signs and to ask and receive upon showing a certificate of survey, signed by the surveyor, a proper deed and proof of ownership under penalty of confiscation." Both at Wiltwijck and Schenectady, the properties measured off included land intended for cultivation, as well as designated for a variety of domestic or agricultural purposes.
19. Ibid. 10.
20. The territory of the patent included the present city of Schenectady, the towns of Rotterdam and Glenville, and part of the town of Niskayuna.
21. Gehring, "Light on New Netherlands: Fort Nassau, Fort Orange and Beverwijck" Also, Joel Munsell, ed. and comp. *The Annals of Albany.* 10 vols. Albany: Joel Munsell. 1850-1859. *Articles of Capitulation,* 28-31.
22. George S. Roberts, *Old Schenectady.* Schenectady: Robson & Adee.
23. Sanders to Pearson, February 20, 1873.
24. Jonathan Pearson, *Genealogies of the First Settlers of Schenectady.* Albany: J. W. Mac Murray, 1883. 189.
25. Sanders to Pearson, February 20, 1873.
26. "D2224, English Confirmatory Patent of 1685, Book of Patents no. 5" 1685. Schenectady County Historical Society.
27. Arnold J. F. van Laer, *Early Records of the City and County of Albany and the Colony of Rensselaerwyck.* Trans. by Jonathan Pearson. Vol. II. Albany: University of the State of New York, 1869-1919. 387.
28. Pearson., First Settlers. 254.
29. Donna Merwick., *Possessing Albany, 1630-1710: The Dutch and English Experiences* Cambridge: Cambridge University Press, 129-130.
30. Ibid. 110. 115.
31. Ibid. 129-130.
32. D2224, ECP.
33. Burke, MF, 38-39. Pearson's division of lands may be too exclusive. By the early 1670's, nearly three miles of land on the east and northern shore of the Mohawk were being used for pasture and the designation of cultivated or uncultivated lands was becoming more obscure.
34. Jonathan Pearson, *History of the Schenectady Patent in the Dutch and English Times, Being Contributions toward a History of the Lower Mohawk Valley.* Albany: J. W. Mac Murray, 1883. Willem Teller's Killetje is today known as the Poenties Kil.
35. Arnold J. F. van Laer, *Early Records of the City and County of Albany and Colony of Rensselaerwyck, Vol. III, Notarial Papers 1 & 2, 1660-1696.* Albany: University of the State of New York, 1918.
36. Ibid.
37. Ibid. 285-287.

38. Jasper Danckaerts and Peter Sluyter, *Journal of a Voyage to New York and a Tour in Several of the American Colonies in 1679-1680.* Trans. and edited. by Henry Cruse Murphy. Brooklyn: Long Island Historical Society, 1867, 315.
39. Susan J. Staffa, *Schenectady Genesis: How a Dutch Colonial Village Became an American City, ca. 1661-1800, Vol. 1, The Colonial Crucible, ca. 1661-1774.* Fleischmann's, N.Y.: Purple Mountain Press, 2004, 74.
40. Edmund B. O'Callaghan and Berthold Fernow, *Documents Relative to the Colonial History of New York. Vol. III.* Albany: Weed, Parsons, 1856-1887, 477.
41. Ibid.
42. M. De Monsignot, Comptroller General of the Marine in Canada to Madam de Maintenon, the morganatic wife of Louis XIV, *Paris Documents, Vol. .IV,* Secretary of State's Office.
43. A livre is a former French money of account and a silver coin, originally equivalent to a pound of silver. It was gradually reduced in value, and replaced by the franc.
44. C. W. van Santvoord, C. S. Halsey, and W. T. Becker. *History of the County of Schenectady.* Schenectady: Barhyte & Birch, 1887. For an artistic interpretation of Schenectady in 1690, reference Len R. Tantillo's painting: *Schenectady Town: A View from Cowhorn Creek, circa. 1690.* 2005. Tantillo's research for this painting is based on Römer's *Plan de Schenectady of 1698.*
45. Joel Munsell, *Annals of Albany. Vol. IX.* Edited and compiled by Joel Munsell. Albany: Joel Munsell, 1850-1859.
46. Deed IV, 209. 20 June 1700. Recorded: 22 April 1701. Willem Teller, grantor to Johannes Teller, grantee. Albany Hall of Records.
47. Burke, MF. 200.
48. Berthold Fernow, comp. *Calendar of Council Minutes, 1668-1783.* Preface by Arnold J. F. van Laer. Introduction by Peter R. Christoph. Harrison, NY: Harbor Hill Books, 1987.
49. Munsell, AA, Vol. IX. Heads of Families in 1697: Schenectady totaled fifty men, forty-one women, one-hundred thirty-three children and fourteen Negroes. Johannes Teller is listed as a head of family in Albany County.
50. George R. Howell and John H. Munsell, *History of the County of Schenectady, New York from 1662 to 1886.* New York: W. W. Munsell & Co., 1886. 37.
51. Staffa, SG, 125.
52. O'Callaghan and Fernow, NYCD, Vol. 4: 874.
53. A similar version of *A Plan of Schenectady* can be found in Pearson's SP, 316. "About 1750, FR. & Ind. Wars" has been added to the title, and the eastern block of Ferry Street, Front Street, Church Street and Union Street appear at a different angle; otherwise, the map appears to be the same as the NYS Library's copy.
54. Isaac Vrooman, *Map of the Town of Schenectady, September, 1768 (A True Copy).* A similar copy of this map was donated to Union College by C. Yates. The original Vrooman map has never been located.
55. Burke, MF, 191.
56. Pearson, *Schenectady Patent,* 31-36. Staffa, *Schenectady Genesis,* 54. A quit-rent, also called a fee-farm rent, is a rent paid by the freeholder on a tract of land and was paid in the products of the land, chiefly wheat. Quit-rents were usually found on manors and not in towns, except Schenectady.
57. D892, Dongan Charter of 1714. SCHS.
58. Munsell, AA, 29.
59. D123, Patent no. 17, Poenties Kil and Mill. SCHS.

60. Will of Johannes Teller. 15 May 1725. To sons, Willem and Jacob, he left the foremost parcel No. 5 over the first creek, to the east of No. 6, being 26 acres and 95 rods, together with the house and lot in the Town of Schenectady, now in his possession, being in length 200 feet. Johannes Teller's original house (Teller-Schermerhorn House) still survives today on a portion of the hindmost parcel, No. 3. The Teller-Schermerhorn House is located at 47 Schermerhorn Road. AHR.
61. Deed "C," 5 November 1817. L. Schermerhorn, grantor, to Nelly Bastiaan, grantee. Schenectady County Clerk's Office.
62. *Dutch Reformed Church Baptism and Marriage Records*. Susanna Teller Vedder was born 25 March 1733 and married Nicholas van Petten in 1749. Susanna Teller Glen was baptized in 1730 and married Abraham van Eps 30 November 1750. SCHS.
63. Jonathan Pearson, Street Book of Deeds. 1660-1800. Reference is to Abraham Yates papers, 1604-1825. NYS Public Library, Manuscripts and Archival Division. SCHS.
64. Ibid.
65. Deed VII, 358-359. Will of William Teller. 9 April 1752. AHR.
66. Deed VII, 39. 8 May 1759. AHR.
67. Deed VII, 254, 6 July 1759. Cornelius Peek is referenced in this deed as the abutting owner on the north of Jellis Fonda. No separately-recorded deed has been located for his parcel. AHR.
68. Mortgage Book VII, 18, 19. 1 May 1782. Recorded: 23 November 1787. While the deed describes Jesse van Slyck as the owner on the east, Mortgage Book V, 11 dated 14 March 1783, recorded 20 March 1783 documents that the owner of record on the east in 1782 was John Sanders, not Jesse van Slyck. AHR.
69. *Marriage Records of the Dutch Reformed Church 1654-1852*. SCHS. *Calendar of Wills, 421*. Harms (Harmanus) Vedder died in 1763, leaving most of his estate to Susanna, his daughter. He devised to his brother, Johannes, a ½ morgen lot purchased from E. Swit and a full half part of his pasture lot lying on the east side of the road that leads from Schenectady to Niskayuna. NYS Library. Annatje Teller died in 1761. 63 Front Street may have been part of her inheritance from Johannes, her deceased brother.
70. Willis T. Hanson, Jr., *A History of Schenectady during the Revolution, to which is appended A Contribution to the Individual Records of the Inhabitants of the Schenectady District during That Period.* Schenectady: Acme Press, 1916. 246.
71. Letter from John Sanders, Jr. to C. V. R. Bonney. July 10, 1875 regarding the Glen genealogy. SCHS.
72. Will Book 33. 434-437. Will of John Sanders. 27 January 1779. Probated: 7 February 1783. *Calendar of Probated Wills: 1671-1815*. NYSA.
73. Mortgage Book V, 11. 14 March 1783. Recorded: 20 March 1783. AHR.
74. Hanson, *History of Schenectady during the Revolution,* 247.
75. Harriet Paige, "*The Diary of Harriet Mumford Paige, Vol. I.*" 186. 187. SCHS.
76. Ibid. 199.
77. *Marriage Records of the First Protestant Dutch Reformed Church* SCHS.
78. *Assessment Roll of the City of Schenectady. Ward 1. 1799. 1800. 1801.* New York State Comptroller's Office Tax Assessment Rolls of Real and Personal Estates. Albany: NYSA.
79. Mortgage V, 11. AHR; Florence A. Christoph, comp. and ed. *Upstate New York in the 1760s: Tax Lists and Selected Militia Rolls of Old Albany County, 1760-1768*. Camden, ME: Picton Press, 1992. 114-122.

80. Mortgage VII, 18, 19. 1 May 1782, R. 23 November 1787. Cornelius P. Van Slyck, mortgagor to John Cuyler, mortgagee. AHR.
81. Christoph, *Upstate New York in the 1760s.* A date of 1766 was assigned to this roll. Nicklaas van Petten, the first husband of Susanna Vedder died in 1762. Susanna Vedder was the daughter of Annatje Teller, Johannes Teller's sister.
82. Record Book of the Committee on Historical Markers. SCHS.
83. Ibid.
84. Ibid.
85. "The Pruyn House." *Colonial Homes* 12, no. 4 July-August 1986: 42-45.
86. Roderic H. Blackburn, "Living with Antiques: The Jesse Van Slyck House in Schenectady, New York." *The Magazine Antiques* August 2003: 75-78.
87. Axel Frieberg "Notebook on the Teller House Restoration." Courtesy of Edward Gifford.
88. Edward Gifford and Edward (Ned) Sutton, Interview by author. Rotterdam, N.Y .17 January 2008. Robbe Stimson also worked as a carpenter on the Teller House.
89. Mortgage Book "B,' 352. 17 May 1813. Cornelius L. Barhydt, mortgagor, to Cornelius Van Vranken, mortgagee. SCCO.
90. Deed "S," 500. 16 September 1839. Abraham van Eps et al, grantor, to Alexander Young, grantee. Schenectady County Clerk's Office.
91. Will of Abraham van Eps, V78, *Calendar of Probated Wills: 1671-1815.* Probated: 16 May 1775. New York State Library.
92. LM430. *1813 Assessment Roll of the City of Schenectady. Ward 1. 1816 Assessment Roll of the City of Schenectady. Ward 1.* SCHS.
93. Staffa, *Schenectady Genesis,* 346-351.
94. Mortgage Book "V," 191. 13 May 1794. Recorded: 4 September 1795. Volekie Veeder, mortgagor to Alexander Ellice, mortgagee. AHR.
95. Pearson, *Genealogies of the First Settlers,* 364-365.
96. Howell and Munsell, *History of the County of Schenectady, N.Y. from 1662 to 1886.* New York: W. W. Munsell & Co., 1886.
97. O'Callaghan and Fernow, NYCD, vol. III: 781, 783, 801.
98. Munsell, AA, vol. X, 182-183.
99. Ibid. 184.
100. Charles Roscoe Canedy III, *Entrepreneurial History of the New York Frontier, 1739-1776.* Ann Arbor: University Microfilms International, 1980.
101. William Johnson, *The Papers of Sir William Johnson.* edited by James A. Sullivan. Vol. I. Albany: University of the State of New York, 1921-1965. 458, 585, 611, 689.
102. Howell and Munsell., *History of the County of Schenectady,* 39.
103. Hanson, *History of Schenectady during the Revolution.* Pension Office Records, John Henry, R4891 and Bartholomew Clute, S 12499.
104. Richard Smith, *A Tour of Four Great Rivers, the Hudson, Mohawk, Susquehanna and Delaware in 1769.* edited by Francis W. Halsey. New York: Charles Scribner's Sons, 1906.
105. Excerpt from the journal of Jabez Maud Fisher. A manuscript copy of his journal is in possession of the Herkimer County Historical Society.
106. Paul Huey and Joseph E. McEvoy. *Report on Archaeological Reconnaissance of the 15-Inch Mohawk River Interceptor Sewer Project.*
107. Will Book "A." 54. Will of William Schermerhorn, Proved. 6 May 1811. SCSC.

108. O'Callaghan and Fernow, NYCD, 10, 677. The eastern angle of the third stockade line was believed to have extended from the present location of the New York Central depot, intersecting with the river at a point not far from the foot of North Street.
109. Unpublished *Memo on the Schenectady Stockade Water Line for the period October 16, 1995 -October 20, 1995.* By permission of Hartgen Archaeological Associates.
110. The Committee on Historic Markers, formed in 1960, designated the date for the Johannes Teller House as1740, based on a reference to the Teller House found in Book "C," 11, November 1817." as being the same house transferred by Johannes Teller to William Schermerhorn in July 1744."
111. Hartgen Archaeological Associates. *Phase 1B Archaeological Investigations for the Schenectady Storm Sewer Expansion of Front Street.* June 1997. 7, 8, 11.
112. Ibid. 8-9.
113. Nelson Greene, *History of the Mohawk Valley: Gateway to the West, 1614-1925.* Vol. I, II Chicago: The S. J. Clarke Publishing Company, 1925.
114. *Assessment Rolls, 1799-1803.*
115. Ibid.
116. Deed Book 29., 438. 9 June 1852, Recorded 10 June 1852. Helena McDougall, Nicholas van Vranken and Harriet Susan Vrooman were Harriet van Vranken's cousins; Nancy (van Vranken) Vrooman was Harriet van Vranken's aunt. Deed Book 32., 19 & 20. 23 April 1853, Recorded 17 July 1854. D. McDougall et al to Harriet Van Vranken. Harmanus I. Vedder is shown as the abutting owner on the east. SCCO.
117. Deed 32, 19 & 20. 23 April 1853. Recorded: 17 July 1854. Harriet van Vranken, grantor to John I. Vedder, grantee. SCCO.
118. Deed. 35, 445. 15 February 1858. Mary Vedder, grantor, to Charles Whitmyer, grantee. SCCO.
119. *Assessment Rolls, 1799-1803. Marriage Records of the Dutch Reformed Church.* SCHS.
120. Mortgage "B," 352. Mortgage discharged 11 July 1814. SCCO.
121. Mortgage V, 191. 13 May 1794, Recorded 4 September 1794. Volekje Veeder, mortgagor to Alexander Ellice, mortgagee. AHR.
122. LM430. Assessment Roll, 1816.
123. Cornelius L. Barheydt had a blacksmithing shop on Front Street. After his wife's death, he went into business with I. I. Yates, under the firm of Yates and Barheydt. The business moved from Front Street to Liberty Street, 2 doors east of the Erie Canal; it specialized in blacksmithing and coach making. They kept an experienced workman at horseshoeing in their employ. *Schenectady Cabinet*, vol. XVII: April 18, 1827.
124. LM430. Assessment Roll, 1816.
125. Pearson, *Genealogies of the First Settlers*, 254-261.
126. "Baptisms of the First Protestant Dutch Church of the City of Schenectady" (1800-1852). SCHS.
127. Records of the Green Street Cemetery. Anna M., wife of Harmanus I. Vedder, died in her 71st year. SCHS.
128. Deed Book 40. 333. 14 August 1862. By will of Harmanus I. Vedder. John L. Hill (John S. Gow, deceased) to Mary S. Gow. House and barn transferred. Lot dimensions: 53' x 41' depth. SCCO.
129. Will Book "G," 307-310. Will of Harmanus I. Vedder. Will made 1 September 1853, Proved 18 June 1856. SCSC.

130. No known deed is recorded in 1862 for the transfer of this lot. However, Mortgage Book 40. 273. Recorded: 3 May 1869. Thomas L. Pemberton, mortgagor, to Daniel Vedder, mortgagee, identifies the house and lot dimensions (39.75‘ from the southwest corner of the house, east to North Street, 66 ‘5 inches to a point 9“ from the barn of John Gow, then west 42’9 inches to the lot of Yourny van Vranken), as spelled out in the will of Harmanus I. Vedder. SCCO.
131. Deed Book 62,. 98. 1 May 1869. Recorded: 3 May 1869. Daniel Vedder, grantor, to Thomas Pemberton, grantee. Thomas Pemberton's wife was Jane Vedder, a cousin of Daniel Vedder. (See Mortgage Book 40, 273. Thomas Pemberton, mortgagor, to Daniel Vedder, mortgagee. 1 May 1869. Recorded: 3 May 1869. SCCO.
132. 1870 Federal Census of the City of Schenectady, Ward 2. 1870 City Directory. SCHS.
133. Deed Book 67, 482. 12 December 1877. E. Cutler, Referee for Jane Pemberton, Franklin J. Pemberton, and Celeste Pemberton and Effringham Putnam to Daniel Vedder. Lot dimensions: 39.75' Frontage, 66'5 inches to point 9" from John Gow's barn, 42'9 inch rear. SCCO.
134. *Schenectady Daily Union, Vol. XI, no. 79 – Vol. XIII.* Tuesday, February 1, 1876 to Thursday, January 31, 1878. "Funeral Notice of Thomas L. Pemberton," 13 April 1877. SCHS.
135. Deed Book 72, 17. 1 March 1881. Mary S. Gow, grantor to Henry L. De Forest, grantee. Lot dimensions: 53' frontage by 41' depth. The barn would later become 5 North Street; the duplex would become 30 North Street. SCCO.
136. *1880 Federal Census of the City of Schenectady, Ward 2.* City Directory, 1880-1888. SCHS.
137. *The Reflector,* August 17, 1882. "Daniel Vedder Obituary," Daniel Vedder died August 9, 1882. By 1848, he had become a partner in the firm of Cornelius S. Groot & Son. After Simon Groot died in 1872, the firm's name was changed to Daniel Vedder & Co.
138. Will Book "L", 227. Will of Daniel Vedder. Will made 18 April 1879. Probated 30 October 1882. SCSC.
139. Twelfth Census of the United State, Schedule No. 1, Population (1900 Federal Census) of the City of Schenectady, Ward 2. Deed Book 87, 379. 15 March 1889. John J. Hart and Alida Hart, grantor, to Alfred Yauchter, grantee. Sale included the barn and frame house. Lot size: 53' x 41'. (5, 7 & 9 North Street). Alfred Yauchter's name is found in the City Directory of 1890, as residing at 5 North Street, the former barn of John S. Gow. SCCO.
140. Ibid. 7 & 9 North Street were still part of Alfred Yauchter's lot in 1900. 7 & 9 North Street was split off from 5 North Street on March 15, 1915 to William Cullen. SCCO.
141. *The New York State Census of 1902 for the City of Schenectady, Ward* 2. SCHS.
142. Will Book "P," 505. Probated will of Deborah Vedder. 3 May 1909. SCSC.
143. Greene, *History of the Mohawk Valley, Vol. II,* 1351, 1443.
144. Deed Book 35, 445. 15 March 1858. Mary Vedder, grantor, to Charles Whitmyer, grantee. Sale of 119 Front Street. Dimensions remained the same as from 1794. 42'6" Frontage to lot of Harmanus I. Vedder, 114'2" North, 38'6" rear to lands of P. Dorsch and south to Front Street. SCCO.
145. Will Book "P," 505. No recorded deed, transferring 121 Front Street from Deborah Vedder to the Home of the Friendless has ever been found, nor is the Home mentioned in Deborah Vedder's will. The Home of the Friendless is today The Heritage Home for Women. SCSC.
146. *Report with Constitution and Bylaws of the Old Ladies Home.* October First, 1909-1910.

147. *Marlette's Schenectady Directory of 1909* shows Charles Judeman's residence as 121 Front Street. *Marlette's Directory of 1910* shows the Hallowell family boarding at 121 Front Street. The *1911 Schenectady Directory* shows Margaret Keeler boarding there. The Federal Census of 1910 shows Charles Judeman as renting 121 Front Street, and Margaret Keeler as residing there. *The Register of Matrons and Inmates* shows Miss Keeler as the matron of the Old Ladies Home from April, 1919 to June, 1921.
148. Will Book "Q," 348. Probated will of Margaret G. Hallowell. November 16, 1910. SCSC.
149. Deed Book 228. 333. April 17, 1918, Recorded May 14, 1918. John Bunyan and Edith Bunyan, et al grantors to George Keeler and Nettie Keeler, grantees. The lot dimensions east 39.75' frontage, 68'5" along North Street, 41'5" rear, south 59'. SCCO.
150. *City Directory of 1918* lists Margaret S. Keeler as matron of the Old Ladies Home. The Federal Census of 1920 lists George, Keeler, his wife, and son as residing at 121 Front Street. Albert Springer is shown on the 1920 and 1930 Federal Census as a tenant of the house. SCHS.
151. Abstract of Title for 121 Front Street. March 10, 1975. Mohawk Abstract Recorded April 23, 1975. John Francis Keeler to Frances H. Keeler. By permission of Marilyn Sassi.
152. Deed Book 987. 370. 16 April 1975, Recorded: 23 April 1975. Frances H. Keeler, individually, and as Administratrix of the Estate of John S. Keeler, deceased, to Axel R. Frieberg. Lot dimensions: From the NW corner of Front and North Street, (68.5 feet, westerly 41.5 feet; south, 59 feet to Front Street, easterly 39.75 feet). SCCO.
153. Edward Gifford, Interview by Hamilton, Claire. The Teller House Restoration of 1976. Rotterdam. (December 2, 2007).
154. Frieberg, "Notes on the Restoration."
155. Ibid.
156. Ibid.
157. Edward Gifford "Notes on the Restoration." January 10, 2007.
158. Edward Gifford, Interview by author, Rotterdam, NY. A VCR tape, filmed by Mary Coffin, Axel Frieberg's lawyer, was made after the restoration was completed. Axel Frieberg describes how he restored the Teller House. Marilyn Sassi, the current owner of the Teller House and an art curator, does not believe the two Delft tiles are authentic to the eighteenth century, but that the remaining Delft tiles are. Walter Wheeler, an architectural historian, and Rod Blackburn, an art curator, believe the tiles are authentic to the mid-eighteenth century.
159. The use of weather boards on the west gable end of the brick Georgian-style house reverted back to a Dutch custom of conserving money on a portion of the house not visible to the street
160. Deed Book 1466, 16. 2 August 1995. The purchase price in the deed is $140,000.00. Edward Gifford believed the sale price was $165,000. SCCO.
161. Deed Book 1554, 313-315. 25 March 1999, Recorded 2 April 1999. SCCO.
162. Deed Book 1612, 264-266. 26 October 2001, Recorded November 13, 2001. SCCO.
163. Deed Book 1423, 879-881. 7 May 2002, Recorded 14 May 2002. SCCO.
164. Ronald. Kingsley, Teller House Property Rescue Project. October 2002. SCCC.
165. Ronald. Kingsley, "Ground Along North Street Reveals Another Mystery." *The Schenectady Spy* 50, *no. 2.* October: 2008.

166. Hon. John Sanders, *Centennial Address Relating to the EARLY HISTORY OF SCHENECTADY and Its First Settlers, Delivered at Schenectady, July 4th, 1876.* Albany: van Benthuysen Printing House, 1879. 39.
167. Deed Book IV, 209. 20 June 1700. Recorded: 22 April 1701. AHR

Index

G

H

I

J

K

L

M